MW00338034

Benchmark Assessments

PROPERTY OF
Cedar Rapids Community
School District

Mc
Graw
Hill
Education

www.mheonline.com/readingwonders

Send all inquiries to:
McGraw-Hill Education
Two Penn Plaza
New York, New York 10121

ISBN: 978-0-07-678305-2
MHID: 0-07-678305-7

Printed in the United States of America.

1 2 3 4 5 6 7 8 9 RHR 20 19 18 17 16 15
A

Table of Contents

Benchmark Assessments

Benchmark Assessments is an integral part of the complete assessment program aligned with *Reading Wonders,* state standards, and advances in summative assessment that feature performance-based tasks, such as the Smarter Balanced Assessment Consortium (SBAC) assessment system.

Purpose of *Benchmark Assessments*

Benchmark Assessments reports on the outcome of student learning and provides summative data in relation to progress through the curriculum. The results of the assessments can be used to inform subsequent instruction, aid in making leveling and grouping decisions, and point toward areas in need of reteaching or remediation. The tests in *Benchmark Assessments* are constructed to mirror the approach and subject concentration found in state-mandated end-of-year and performance-based assessments, such as the SBAC End of Year (EOY) English Language Arts (ELA) test and SBAC performance-based assessments. Student performance in these assessments can act as a signal of student readiness for the demands of high-stakes testing as well as a snapshot of student progress toward end-of-year goals.

Focus of *Benchmark Assessments*

The tests focus on the following key areas of ELA:

- Comprehension of literature and informational text
- Using text features to access or clarify information
- Vocabulary acquisition and use
- Research skills
- Drafting, editing, and revising text
- Command of the conventions of standard English language
- Writing to sources within the parameters of specific genres

Assessment Items Featured in *Benchmark Assessments*

Benchmark assessments feature the following item types—selected response (SR), multiple selected response (MSR), evidence-based selected response (EBSR), constructed response (CR), technology-enhanced items (TE), and Performance Tasks (PT). (Please note that the print versions of TE items are available in this component; the full functionality of the items is available only through the online assessment.) This variety of item types provides multiple methods of assessing student understanding, allows for deeper investigation into skills and strategies, and provides students an opportunity to become familiar with the kinds of items and approaches they will encounter in high-stakes assessments.

Teacher Introduction

Overview of *Benchmark Assessments*

The *Benchmark Assessments* component consists of three tests—Benchmark Test 1, Benchmark Test 2, and Benchmark Test 3.

Test 1 focuses on key skills that are part of the instruction in Units 1–3, Test 2 samples key skills from Units 1–6, and Test 3 features a suite of PTs.

Test 1 and Test 2 feature **39** items that mirror the focus and presentation students will encounter in end-of-year testing. The tests are broken into two sessions. A listening comprehension section has been omitted from the print component so as to allow for ease of administration. One online version of Test 2 contains a listening comprehension section that can be administered, if you feel students will benefit from the experience.

Test 3 contains examples of PTs that are part of traditional performance-based assessment.

- Narrative
  - Students craft a narrative using information from the sources.
- Informational
  - Students generate a thesis based on the sources and use information from the sources to explain this thesis.
- Opinion
  - Students analyze the ideas in sources and make a claim that they support using the sources.

Each PT assesses standards that address comprehension, research skills, genre writing, and the use of standard English language conventions (ELC). The stimulus texts and research questions in each task build toward the goal of the final writing topic.

Administering *Benchmark Assessments*

Benchmark Test 1 should be given to students after Unit 3 is completed. Benchmark 2 should be given to students close to the end of the year or before students take their EOY test. The PTs in Test 3 can be administered at various times during the year. The Narrative Task can be given at the start of the year and again closer to the performance-based assessment date to measure student growth and test readiness.

Due to the length of the test (and to provide students a test-taking experience that is in concert with standardized testing), the schedule below is suggested. (Session 1 and Session 2 can be spaced over two days or grouped together with a short break in between.)

- Session 1 of Tests 1 and 2—45 to 60 minutes
- Session 2 of Tests 1 and 2—35 to 50 minutes
- PTs in Test 3—90 to 100 minutes. (Provide students 30 to 40 minutes to read the stimulus materials and answer the research questions, and 60 to 70 minutes for planning, writing, and editing their responses. If desired, provide students a short break between these activities.)

Teacher Introduction

Scoring *Benchmark Assessments*

Items 1–39 in Tests 1 and 2 are each worth two points, for a 78-point assessment. Each part of an EBSR is worth 1 point; MSR and TE items should be answered correctly in full, though you may choose to provide partial credit. For written responses, use the correct response parameters provided in the Answer Key and the scoring rubrics listed below to assign a score.

Short Response Score: 2

The response is well-crafted and concise and shows a thorough understanding of the underlying skill. Appropriate text evidence is used to answer the question.

Short Response Score: 1

The response shows partial understanding of the underlying skill. Text evidence is featured, though examples are too general.

Each PT is a 15-point assessment. For PT full-writes, use the rubrics on the following pages. Score the task holistically on a 10-point scale: 4 points for purpose/organization [P/O]; 4 points for evidence/elaboration [E/E] or development/elaboration [D/E]; and 2 points for English language conventions [C].

Evaluating Scores

The goal of each test is to evaluate student mastery of previously-taught material and to gauge preparedness for state-mandated testing.

Test 1 can serve as a summative, mid-year assessment.

Test 2 can serve as a summative, EOY assessment.

The PTs that comprise Test 3 can be assigned at points directly following specific instruction in the task genre to assess student mastery.

The expectation is for students

- to score 80% or higher on Tests 1 and 2; and
- to score "12" or higher on each PT.

For students who do not meet these benchmarks, assign appropriate lessons from the Tier 2 online PDFs. Use student results in particular test categories to guide intervention.

Teacher Introduction

Use the rubrics to score the task holistically on a 10-point scale:
4 points for purpose/organization [P/O]; 4 points for evidence/elaboration [E/E] or development/elaboration [D/E]; and 2 points for English language conventions [C]

Unscorable or **Zero** responses are unrelated to the topic, illegible, contain little or no writing, or show little to no command of the conventions of standard English.

INFORMATIVE PERFORMANCE TASK SCORING RUBRIC

Score	Purpose/Organization	Evidence/Elaboration	Conventions
4	• **effective** organizational structure • clear statement of main idea based on purpose, audience, task • consistent use of various transitions • logical progression of ideas	• **convincing** support for main idea; **effective** use of sources • integrates comprehensive evidence from sources • relevant references • effective use of elaboration • audience-appropriate domain-specific vocabulary	
3	• **evident** organizational structure • adequate statement of main idea based on purpose, audience, task • adequate, somewhat varied use of transitions • adequate progression of ideas	• **adequate** support for main idea; **adequate** use of sources • some integration of evidence from sources • references may be general • adequate use of some elaboration • generally audience-appropriate domain-specific vocabulary	
2	• **inconsistent** organizational structure • unclear or somewhat unfocused main idea • inconsistent use of transitions with little variety • formulaic or uneven progression of ideas	• **uneven** support for main idea; **limited** use of sources • weakly integrated, vague, or imprecise evidence from sources • references are vague or absent • weak or uneven elaboration • uneven domain-specific vocabulary	• **adequate** command of spelling, capitalization, punctuation, grammar, and usage • few errors
1	• **little or no** organizational structure • few or no transitions • frequent extraneous ideas; may be formulaic • may lack introduction and/or conclusion • confusing or ambiguous focus; may be very brief	• **minimal** support for main idea; **little or no** use of sources • minimal, absent, incorrect, or irrelevant evidence from sources • references are absent or incorrect • minimal, if any, elaboration • limited or ineffective domain-specific vocabulary	• **partial** command of spelling, capitalization, punctuation, grammar, and usage • some patterns of errors

Teacher Introduction

NARRATIVE PERFORMANCE TASK SCORING RUBRIC

Score	Purpose/Organization	Development/Elaboration	Conventions
4	• **fully sustained** organization; **clear** focus • effective, unified plot • effective development of setting, characters, point of view • transitions clarify relationships between and among ideas • logical sequence of events • effective opening and closing	• **effective** elaboration with details, dialogue, description • clear expression of experiences and events • effective use of relevant source material • effective use of various narrative techniques • effective use of sensory, concrete, and figurative language	
3	• **adequately sustained** organization; **generally maintained** focus • evident plot with loose connections • adequate development of setting, characters, point of view • adequate use of transitional strategies • adequate sequence of events • adequate opening and closing	• **adequate** elaboration with details, dialogue, description • adequate expression of experiences and events • adequate use of source material • adequate use of various narrative techniques • adequate use of sensory, concrete, and figurative language	
2	• **somewhat sustained** organization; **uneven** focus • inconsistent plot with evident flaws • uneven development of setting, characters, point of view • uneven use of transitional strategies, with little variety • weak or uneven sequence of events • weak opening and closing	• **uneven** elaboration with **partial** details, dialogue, description • uneven expression of experiences and events • vague, abrupt, or imprecise use of source material • uneven, inconsistent use of narrative technique • partial or weak use of sensory, concrete, and figurative language	• **adequate** command of spelling, capitalization, punctuation, grammar, and usage • few errors
1	• **basic** organization; **little or no** focus • little or no discernible plot; may just be a series of events • brief or no development of setting, characters, point of view • few or no transitional strategies • little or no organization of event sequence; extraneous ideas • no opening and/or closing	• **minimal** elaboration with **few or no** details, dialogue, description • confusing expression of experiences and events • little or no use of source material • minimal or incorrect use of narrative techniques • little or no use of sensory, concrete, and figurative language	• **partial** command of spelling, capitalization, punctuation, grammar, and usage • some patterns of errors

Teacher Introduction

OPINION PERFORMANCE TASK SCORING RUBRIC			
Score	**Purpose/Organization**	**Evidence/Elaboration**	**Conventions**
4	• **effective** organizational structure; **sustained** focus • consistent use of various transitions • logical progression of ideas • effective introduction and conclusion • clearly communicated opinion for purpose, audience, task	• **convincing** support/evidence for main idea; **effective** use of sources; **precise** language • comprehensive evidence from sources is integrated • relevant, specific references • effective elaborative techniques • appropriate domain-specific vocabulary for audience, purpose	
3	• **evident** organizational structure; **adequate** focus • adequate use of transitions • adequate progression of ideas • adequate introduction and conclusion • clear opinion, mostly maintained, though loosely • adequate opinion for purpose, audience, task	• **adequate** support/evidence for main idea; **adequate** use of sources; **general** language • some evidence from sources is integrated • general, imprecise references • adequate elaboration • generally appropriate domain-specific vocabulary for audience, purpose	
2	• **inconsistent** organizational structure; **somewhat sustained** focus • inconsistent use of transitions • uneven progression of ideas • introduction or conclusion, if present, may be weak • somewhat unclear or unfocused opinion	• **uneven** support for main idea; **partial** use of sources; **simple** language • evidence from sources is weakly integrated, vague, or imprecise • vague, unclear references • weak or uneven elaboration • uneven or somewhat ineffective use of domain-specific vocabulary for audience, purpose	• **adequate** command of spelling, capitalization, punctuation, grammar, and usage • few errors
1	• **little or no** organizational structure or focus • few or no transitions • frequent extraneous ideas are evident; may be formulaic • introduction and/or conclusion may be missing • confusing opinion	• **minimal** support for main idea; **little or no** use of sources; **vague** language • source material evidence is minimal, incorrect, or irrelevant • references absent or incorrect • minimal, if any, elaboration • limited or ineffective use of domain-specific vocabulary for audience, purpose	• **partial** command of spelling, capitalization, punctuation, grammar, and usage • some patterns of errors

Teacher Introduction

Answer Keys in *Benchmark Assessments*

The Answer Keys have been constructed to provide the information needed to aid understanding of student performance.

Correct answers, content focus, standards alignment, and complexity information are listed.

15	B, E	Main Idea and Key Details	RI.5.2	DOK 2
16	D	Context Clues	L.5.4a	DOK 2
17A	C	Main Idea and Key Details	RI.5.2	DOK 2
17B	B	Main Idea and Key Details/Text Evidence	RI.5.2/RI.5.1	DOK 2

Scoring tables show distinct categories to pinpoint possible areas of intervention or enrichment.

Comprehension: Selected Response 1A, 1B, 2A, 2B, 4, 6A, 6B, 7A, 7B, 8A, 8B, 10, 12, 13, 21A, 21B, 23A, 23B, 24A, 24B, 27, 28, 29A, 29B, 30A, 30B, 32, 33	/34	%
Comprehension: Constructed Response 5, 28	/4	%
Vocabulary 3A, 3B, 9A, 9B, 11, 22A, 22B, 25A, 25B, 26, 31A, 31B	/14	%
Research 14, 15, 16, 17	/8	%
Drafting, Editing, Revising 18, 19, 20, 37, 38, 39	/12	%
English Language Conventions 34, 35, 36	/6	%
Total Benchmark Assessment Score	/78	%

For PTs, SR items are worth 1 point each. CR items are worth 2 points each. Use the rubrics to score the full-write. An anchor paper response can be found for each PT. This top-line response is included to assist with scoring.

Narrative Performance Task				
Question	**Answer**	**CCSS**	**Complexity**	**Score**
1	B, D		DOK 3	/1
2	see below	RI.5.1, RI.5.2, RI.5.7, RI.5.8, RI.5.9 W.5.2, W.5.3a–e, W.5.4, W.5.7 L.5.1, L.5.2	DOK 3	/2
3	see below		DOK 3	/2
Story	see below		DOK 4	/4 [P/O] /4 [D/E] /2 [C]
Total Score				/15

SESSION 1

Read the text. Then answer the questions.

The Problem of Pickles

Shakira had always wanted a dog, but her family had never been able to have one. They moved a lot because of Shakira's mother's job, and sometimes they lived in places that didn't allow pets.

Right now the family was living in central Iowa; they had a big house with a yard. Shakira thought her dream might finally come true. She saw a newspaper listing for puppies in need of homes, and she fell instantly in love with the profile of an adorable little mutt named Meadow, but when Shakira shared the description of Meadow with her parents, their expressions darkened.

"I'm sorry, sweetie," said her mother sadly. "I want a dog, too, but we'll probably only be in this house for a year before my next promotion. By the time you start junior high school, we should be in one place for good, and then I promise you we'll get a wonderful dog."

The next day, Shakira was sitting at a table in the school cafeteria with her friend Zoe, whose family was in the same boat: Zoe's mother was a sergeant in the military, so she had to relocate a lot, as well.

Instead of laughing and talking a mile a minute as they usually did, both girls sat staring glumly at the mac and cheese on their plates.

"What's wrong?" asked Zoe.

"I have the same old problem as always," sighed Shakira. "I want a puppy, but my parents say we can't get one until we stop moving, and that won't be for a few more years. What is bothering you?"

"My situation is even worse," sighed Zoe. "I have the absolute greatest dog in the world, but the military is sending my mom overseas to Germany for six months. I have to move in with my grandmother. Grandma lives in a town house that doesn't allow pets, so we might have to give Pickles up for adoption—forever!" Zoe cried and dabbed at her tears with a napkin.

"That's terrible!" exclaimed Shakira sympathetically, but then a light bulb went off in her head. "But wait, what if my family and I take care of Pickles while your mom is away? We'll be here until at least June, much more than six months, we have a fenced yard, and I would take such good care of her!"

GO ON →

Zoe stopped crying, but her expression was still sad as she said, "Knowing that I wouldn't have to say good-bye to Pickles forever would mean a lot, but I'll still have to go months and months without seeing her because my grandmother lives far away, in Connecticut. It will be just terrible to miss my mom and my dog at the same time!"

A light shone in Shakira's eyes and she laughed, saying "Maybe you can still see Pickles! We have a camera on our computer that we use when we call my grandparents. I could use it to call you every day after school, and you could see Pickles online!"

"Wow!" said Zoe. "That sounds perfect."

That night at dinner, Shakira took a deep breath before presenting her plan to her parents. She explained that she wanted to adopt a dog temporarily for a friend whose mother was a soldier, and that the dog was house-trained, well-behaved, and it would need a home for just six months.

"That way I get to enjoy a dog while we're here in Iowa, and Zoe doesn't have to lose her best friend in the whole world!"

She held her breath while her parents looked at each other.

Then her mom smiled and said, "That is a wonderful plan, Shakira. Since your friend's mother is sacrificing a great deal for our country, we would be proud to help her. But are you sure you will be okay giving up this dog when the time comes?"

Shakira nodded and said, "It may be hard, but I'll be happy knowing that Pickles is back with Zoe. Besides, I can always visit with her online!"

GO ON →

Name: _____ Date: _____

1 The following question has two parts. First, answer part A. Then, answer part B.

Part A: Read the sentence from the text.

She explained that she wanted to adopt a dog temporarily for a friend whose mother was a soldier, and that the dog was house-trained, well behaved, and it would need a home for just six months.

What is the meaning of the word temporarily as it is used in the sentence?

(A) for a short time

(B) as soon as possible

(C) when the time comes

(D) for as long as necessary

Part B: Which detail from the text **best** supports your answer in part A?

(A) "we should be in one place for good, and then I promise you we'll get a wonderful dog."

(B) "we might have to give Pickles up for adoption—forever!"

(C) "I could use it to call you every day"

(D) "it would need a home for just six months."

2 Draw a line from each character to the way she responds to the main problem in the text.

Shakira		worried about the challenges of raising Pickles
Shakira's mother		able to make hard choices in order to keep Pickles forever
Zoe		willing to overcome problems to get what she wants

GO ON →

3 The following question has two parts. First, answer part A. Then, answer part B.

Part A: Which sentence **best** identifies the theme of the text?

(A) Friends can plan together to find what is best for everyone.

(B) A single dog can bring happiness to many different children.

(C) Everyone should help the families of soldiers when possible.

(D) People who move a lot should not have pets.

Part B: Which sentence from the text **best** supports your answer in part A?

(A) "'I could use it to call you every day after school, and you could see Pickles online!'"

(B) "'That way I get to enjoy a dog while we're here in Iowa, and Zoe doesn't have to lose her best friend in the whole world!'"

(C) "'Since your friend's mother is sacrificing a great deal for our country, we would be proud to help her.'"

(D) "'But are you sure you will be okay giving up this dog when the time comes?'"

4 Describe how the characters solve their problem. Use details from the text to support your answer.

_____

_____

_____

_____

_____

_____

GO ON →

5 How have events in the lives of Shakira and Zoe been different, and how have they been alike?

(A) Zoe has a pet and Shakira does not; both move because of their mothers' jobs.

(B) Shakira has lived in Iowa a long time, Zoe has not; both have to live with their grandmothers from time to time.

(C) Shakira's situation is worse than Zoe's; both attend the same school.

(D) Zoe has a dog and Shakira doesn't; They both have big backyards for pets to play in.

GO ON →

Read the text. Then answer the questions.

The Dust Bowl

On April 14, 1935, many people in the Southern Plains of the United States feared the world was coming to an end. A dense black cloud sped toward them like a giant locomotive. It reached from the ground more than 100 feet into the sky. But it was not a rain cloud.

It was made up of millions of particles of fine dust, a thick blanket that blocked out the sun. Everyone rushed to get inside so they would not choke on the dirt. Winds of more than 60 miles per hour drove the dust against cars and buildings. It came into houses through the tiniest cracks, even when the doors and windows were closed and locked. That day was called "Black Sunday." It brought the worst of the storms in the area called the Dust Bowl.

Wheat Will Win the War!

During and after World War I, from about 1917–1930, there was a great demand for wheat. Wheat is used to make flour for bread and other products. Huge areas of farmland in Europe were destroyed by the fighting there. People around the world needed wheat from the United States.

The United States government announced that "Wheat Will Win the War!" Americans and their allies would be well fed while their opponents did not have enough food. Farmers knew they could sell all the wheat they raised, and at fair prices.

The Southern Plains offered a perfect spot for wheat farms. The land was flat and covered with low grass and shrubs. With new, powerful tractors, farmers could plow under the grass, leaving the soil ready for planting long, straight rows of wheat. So many people began to grow wheat that some called the period The Great Plow-Under. There was a great demand for American beef, too, as cattle ranchers increased the size of their herds. The cattle ate so much of the grass that the land was almost as bare as the land for planting wheat.

Drought and Dust

The Southern Plains was a great place to farm, but in 1931, everything changed. It simply stopped raining. One dry year led into the next. It was not until 1939 that regular rains began again. By that time, much of the soil had blown away.

GO ON →

Without rain to grow wheat and grass, the upper layer of soil became dry and dusty. There were few trees and plants to hold down this layer. So when the wind raced across the flat fields, the soil was easily blown away. Dust storms became common during the 1930s.

During this period, adults and children wore face masks outside to keep the dust out of their mouths and lungs. Many people became sick and some died from "dust pneumonia" triggered when they breathed in too much dust. Animals in fields died when their stomachs filled with dust.

After years of dust storms, with no crops or income, many people left their farms. They abandoned their land and moved away. They had little money and few household possessions. By the end of the period, one-fourth of all the people had left the area. So many people went to California that guards were sent to the state's borders to try to keep them out.

Government Action

Hugh Bennett was the head of the United States government agency that tried to protect farmland. He had struck out in his earlier attempts to get the government to take action, however, the "Black Sunday" storm reached into the Midwest and East. When the storm hid the sun in Washington, D.C., Bennett announced to Congress, "This, gentlemen, is what I have been talking about."

Congress passed the Soil Conservation Act soon afterward. The government paid farmers to change their methods of farming so that the topsoil could not be so easily blown away. Farmers rotated their crops and plowed the land in curves instead of straight lines. They also planted trees to slow down the wind. These and other methods reduced by 65% the amount of soil blown away.

The Future

Once the rains returned in 1939, much of the Southern Plains gradually returned to valuable farmland. Some land is still barren and dusty. There is currently no way to prevent a drought. Modern farming techniques, however, are able to prevent the return of the Black Blizzards of the 1930s.

GO ON →

6 The following question has two parts. First, answer part A. Then, answer part B.

Part A: Read the sentence from the text.

A dense black cloud sped toward them <u>like a giant locomotive.</u>

What effect does the author create by using this simile?

(A) a sense of curiosity

(B) a sense of danger

(C) a sense of wonder

(D) a sense of mystery

Part B: Which sentence from the text **best** supports your answer in part A?

(A) "But it was not a rain cloud."

(B) "It was made up of millions of particles of fine dust"

(C) "Winds of more than 60 miles per hour drove the dust"

(D) "It came into houses through the tiniest cracks"

GO ON →

7 Read the sentence from the text.

Congress passed the Soil Conservation Act soon afterward.

What led Congress to pass this act?

(A) the dust storm that reached the Midwest and East

(B) the many people who moved to California

(C) the early attempts of Hugh Bennet to protect farmland

(D) the deaths of animals in the fields

8 Read the sentence from the text.

After years of dust storms, with no crops or income, many people abandoned their land and moved west.

Indicate the words or phrases that have the same meaning as the word abandoned. Choose **two** options.

(A) sold

(B) had left

(C) had little

(D) went to

(E) were sent

(F) keep them out

GO ON →

9 Read the sentence from the text.

Modern farming <u>techniques</u>, however, are able to prevent the return of the Black Blizzards of the 1930s.

The word <u>techniques</u> means "methods or ways of doing things." Which **three** phrases from the text are examples of farming <u>techniques</u>?

(A) "sell all the wheat they raised"

(B) "wore face masks"

(C) "abandoned their land"

(D) "rotated their crops"

(E) "plowed the land in curves instead of straight lines"

(F) "planted trees to slow down the wind"

10 The following question has two parts. First, answer part A. Then, answer part B.

Part A: Which statement best describes the problem that World War I caused the people of the Southern Plains?

(A) The war destroyed huge areas of American farmland.

(B) The war forced the people to plow under their wheat crops.

(C) The war caused a need for food that the people met by growing more wheat.

(D) The war caused the people to feed their extra wheat to larger herds of cattle.

Part B: Which sentence from the text **best** supports your answer in part A?

(A) "During and after World War I, from about 1917–1930, there was a great demand for wheat."

(B) "Farmers knew they could sell all the wheat they raised, and at fair prices."

(C) "So many people began to grow wheat that some called the period The Great Plow-Under."

(D) "There was a great demand for American beef, too, as cattle ranchers increased the size of their herds."

GO ON →

11 The following question has two parts. First, answer part A. Then, answer part B.

Part A: Which conclusion can be made about the author's opinion of the people of the Dust Bowl?

Ⓐ The author believes the people were not willing to work hard.

Ⓑ The author believes the people were proud to live in the Southern Plains.

Ⓒ The author sees the people as suffering from the damage to their environment.

Ⓓ The author sees the people as tough cattle ranchers and stubborn farmers.

Part B: Which sentence from the text **best** supports your answer in part A?

Ⓐ "It simply stopped raining."

Ⓑ "So many people went to California that guards were sent to the state's border to keep them out."

Ⓒ "They had little money and few household possessions."

Ⓓ "After years of dust storms, with no crops or income, many people abandoned their land and moved west."

GO ON →

12 The following question has two parts. First, answer part A. Then, answer part B.

Part A: Which statement **best** summarizes the main idea of the text?

Ⓐ The Dust Bowl led to new farming practices.

Ⓑ Congress helped to solve the problems in the Dust Bowl.

Ⓒ The return of drought to the Southern Plains remains a threat.

Ⓓ The Dust Bowl greatly affected farms on the Southern Plains.

Part B: Which sentence from the text **best** supports your answer in part A?

Ⓐ "Congress passed the Soil Conservation Act soon afterward."

Ⓑ "These and other methods reduced by 65% the amount of soil blown away."

Ⓒ "There is currently no way to prevent a drought."

Ⓓ "Dust storms become common during the 1930s."

13 How does the author organize the section "Drought and Dust"?

Ⓐ by stating the pros and cons of raising wheat

Ⓑ by tracing the causes and effects of dust storms

Ⓒ tracing the causes and effects of droughts

Ⓓ listing in importance the characteristics of an effective leader

GO ON →

Read the directions. Then answer the questions.

14 A student is writing a research report about the Mars *Curiosity* Rover, and she has found a source. Read **Source 1** and the directions that follow.

Source 1

The Mars *Curiosity* Rover is part of NASA's Mars Exploration Program: a multi-year effort to explore Mars using robots. Earlier Mars rovers cost about $1 billion; *Curiosity* cost over $2.5 billion. *Curiosity* is looking for tiny forms of life called microbes. The rover carries instruments to study the soil and rocks on Mars.

The robot is trying to learn whether the planet is fit for life. It has a lab to carry out experiments and send information back to Earth. The rover will likely find life. Even if no life is found, the project is worth the expense.

The student found information about the Mars *Curiosity* Rover in a second source. Which sentences from the second source support the author's opinion in **Source 1**? Select **two** options.

(A) Over its nine-year life, *Curiosity* will cost each American just $8.

(B) Despite some budget cuts, NASA has a budget of more than $17 billion.

(C) The mission·of *Curiosity* is to find evidence that Mars supported life in the past.

(D) In December 2014, the *Curiosity* Rover discovered evidence of water on Mars, and where there is water there is life.

(E) When the first close-up pictures of Mars were published in 1965, NASA knew it had to start a Mars exploration program.

(F) Like all Mars Exploration Program missions, future missions will be driven by science-based questions that come from information gained from earlier missions.

GO ON →

A student made a plan for a research report. Read the plan and the directions that follow.

Research Report Plan
Topic: Mars *Curiosity* Rover
Audience: students at my school
Purpose: to inform
Research Question: How will *Curiosity* find evidence of life on Mars?

The student found a source for the research report. Read the source. Then complete the sentence.

(1) The Mars *Curiosity* Rover is part of NASA's Mars Exploration Program: a multi-year effort to explore Mars using robots. (2) Earlier Mars rovers cost about $1 billion; *Curiosity* cost over $2.5 billion. (3) *Curiosity* is looking for tiny forms of life called microbes. (4) The rover carries instruments to study the soil and rocks on Mars.

(5) The robot is trying to learn if the planet is fit for life. (6) It has a lab to carry out experiments and send information back to Earth. (7) The rover will likely find life. (8) Even if no life is found, the project is worth the expense.

Which sentences from the source **best** answer the research question? Select **two** choices.

(A) Sentence 1
(B) Sentence 2
(C) Sentence 3
(D) Sentence 4
(E) Sentence 5
(F) Sentence 6

GO ON →

16 A student needs to write a report about tropical plants that are easy to grow.

Research Report Plan
Topic: Tropical Plants
Audience: first-time gardeners
Purpose: to inform
Research Question: What tropical plants are easy to grow?

Which of these books is **most likely** a useful source for the information needed to write the report?

(A) *Adventures in the Tropical Jungles*

(B) *Tropical Plants: New Medical Discoveries*

(C) *The Tropical Garden: A Beginner's Guide*

(D) *Tropical Flowers and Trees of the Amazon*

17 A student is writing a report about the history of air travel. The student found the following sources. Which website is **most likely** a useful source of information for the report?

(A) a website offering travel discounts

(B) a website of a major airline company

(C) a website about transportation in the past

(D) a website comparing air travel in various countries

GO ON →

18 A student is writing a report for a teacher about proper tooth and gum care. Read the introduction of the report and the student's notes. Then complete the task.

Taking care of your teeth and gums is called dental hygiene, and it is important because it can prevent tooth decay and gum disease. Good dental hygiene has other benefits, too. It can keep you from having bad breath and make your smile look nicer. According to dentists, there are some ways in which you can take care of your teeth and prevent diseases and cavities. These include brushing and flossing every day, eating healthy foods, and visiting a dentist regularly.

Student notes:
- Floss once a day.
- Brush twice a day—30 minutes after eating.
- Plaque on teeth has bacteria—causes cavities if they come in contact with food.
- Visit dentist for a cleaning (every 6 months).
- Use toothpaste (pea-size drop) and soft bristle toothbrush.
- Candy/other sugary foods: make more acids in the mouth; can damage teeth.
- Plaque hardens into tartar (when on teeth too long)—only dentist can remove it.
- Brush the fronts and backs of all the teeth; also the crevices between the teeth.
- Flossing: gets rid of plaque and food between teeth.
- Avoid sugary snacks (or brush after eating them).
- Not flossing: tartar builds up on the teeth.

Write the body of a report that groups related information from the student's notes together.

_____

_____

_____

_____

_____

_____

GO ON →

19 A student is writing an opinion essay for the school newspaper about a volunteer program at her school. The student wants to revise the draft so that all the details support the opinion. Read the draft of the opinion essay. Then complete the task that follows.

Recently the school has proposed starting one of two volunteer programs. We can either start a program that lets students train future assistance dogs, or we can start a reading buddies group. I believe that the first choice is the better one. Assistance dogs help people with disabilities complete daily tasks, and this gives these people more independence. Dogs can help people get around more easily or alert them to potential dangers. Helping train assistance dogs would be a big responsibility for a kid. Plus, what student wouldn't love playing with an adorable, lovable puppy?

Choose the **best** replacement for the underlined sentence in order to support the student's opinion.

(A) Teaching assistance dogs how to do things for people would be an interesting job for a kid to have.

(B) Training an assistance dog would teach a kid the importance of doing a good job and be fun at the same time.

(C) Kids may have trouble raising and training a puppy, but if they do, they can ask their parents to help them.

(D) Many assistance dogs are Labradors, but if kids are allergic to them, they may choose a breed such as a poodle.

GO ON →

20 A student is writing a narrative for class about learning a new game. The student wants to revise the draft to include a conclusion. Read the draft of the narrative. Then answer the question that follows.

One Saturday, Carly and I were watching cartoons when Mom came in and stood in front of the TV. She said, "I can't believe you'd rather sit inside instead of playing outside on a beautiful day!" Then she flipped the TV off. "When I was your age, I was outside playing Kick the Can."

"Kick the Can?" Carly asked, confused. "What's that?"

Smiling, Mom told us to follow her outside. I found an empty coffee can from the recycling bin, Carly rounded up the kids on our block, Mom explained the rules, and we spent the next two hours playing.

Which sentence is the **best** ending for the narrative?

Ⓐ Although we still watch TV, we did not like playing Kick the Can.

Ⓑ When we finished playing, we agreed the game was too dangerous for us.

Ⓒ At the end of the game, Carly and I promised Mom we would never watch TV again.

Ⓓ After that exciting afternoon with our friends, Carly and I play kick the can every Saturday.

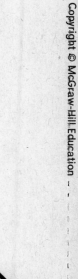

STOP

SESSION 2

Read the text. Then answer the questions.

Ant Farm

Murphy's dad ran an excavating business. "Basically, this meant that he dug big holes," Murphy's older brother once told him. That line caused his dad to chuckle. But when Murphy was really little, watching his dad operate an excavator was his favorite thing in the whole world!

He loved the big yellow machines with their sticks and buckets and giant wheels; he admired the smooth way they turned around, and the way his dad could open and close the huge shovel from inside his cab. The best part was when his father used the excavator to pick up a giant rock as easily as if it were a tiny pebble.

When Murphy was three, his dad made him a video of the excavator in action, and Murphy used to watch it over and over until everyone in the family begged him to switch to something else.

Now that he was ten, Murphy had added to his list of interests.

He liked soccer and math. He had an ant farm, and he was excellent at electronic games. He had lots of friends. But sometimes on summer days, Murphy would accompany his father to a job site and watch a little excavation.

One July morning, Murphy was sitting at the desk in his bedroom, slurping down cereal and watching his ants. The farm was actually a big clear plastic box, and through the sides he could observe the insects making complicated tunnels and using their antennae to communicate. For the first time, it occurred to him that the ants were excavators, too.

"Murph," his father called from the foot of the stairs, "I'm going on a new assignment today. We're digging foundations for a housing development out in Fitchburg. Want to tag along?"

Murphy jumped up and said, "Bye, ants," and as he started to turn away, he could swear that one of the ants waved his feelers at Murphy. Sometimes it really felt as if he and the ants were talking to each other!

When they reached the job site, Dad looked around for a spot from which his son could watch the action. He always called this the Surveillance Circle, even though it wasn't really a circle; this time it was an upward-sloping, narrow piece of ground. It was a safe distance away from the area marked out for the foundation.

GO ON →

Dad knew that construction could be a dangerous business, and he made sure Murphy knew it, too. Murphy understood that if he ever ran onto the field near the machines, he would never get to come along again.

Murphy watched in anticipation as his father started up the excavator and began driving toward a marked-out area. This was the moment he had been looking forward to all morning. The other workers moved to a safe distance, and carefully observed his father. When his father arrived at the right spot, the engine roared. The machine's arm extended, the digger lowered, and Murphy waited for the first big satisfying scoop of dirt.

Instead, there was a loud, clanging noise like a toddler banging on a metal pot with a spoon. Instead of carving deeply into the ground, the excavator bounced along the surface. Dad tried the move again, but this time it made a louder clang.

Murphy was on pins and needles trying to figure out what was going on, but he knew better than to leave his post. When a tall man in a hard hat walked out to talk to his dad, Murphy could hear a few words of their conversation: "solid bedrock" . . . "find just the right spot" . . . "expensive!"

Something tickled Murphy's right leg. It was an ant. Murphy gently blew it away, but the ant turned back and tickled his leg again with its feelers. Curiously, Murphy bent over until his eyes were nearly level with the tiny creature, which was waving its feelers frantically as if trying to send the boy a message. Maybe it came from watching his ants at home for so long, but Murphy suddenly felt as if he could understand! The ant was waving its antennae in a certain direction. Murphy stood up and waved his arms in the air to get his father's attention. His father stuck his head out of the cab and yelled, "What is it?"

Murphy cupped his hands together to make his voice carry.

"Try backing up a little," he called. "I think you'll find a better spot to dig."

Dad stared for a second, looking baffled. Then he muttered, "Why not?" He backed up the excavator about five feet. The bucket swung through the air, dipped, and cut smoothly into the ground.

Murphy watched as Dad wiggled the bucket around. It reminded him of when he was six or seven and trying to extract one of his baby teeth that was about to come out.

Slowly the bucket rose up, removing the most gigantic rock Murphy had ever seen. Cheers broke out from all of the workers.

GO ON →

Later, Murphy's father asked, "How on Earth did you know I should approach that spot from a few feet back? That was weird."

Murphy thought hard. Should he open up and tell his father that he could understand insects? He decided against it. "I just, er, saw something," he mumbled.

"It's a good thing," his father said. "You just saved the boss a lot of money and earned me a bonus at the same time. I think you should get something out of this, too. Do you have any requests?"

"Ummm," said Murphy, "there's this new kind of ant farm . . . "

"If you say so, buddy," laughed his father.

GO ON →

21 The following question has two parts. First, answer part A. Then, answer part B.

Part A: Read the sentence from the text.

"He always called this the Surveillance Circle, even though it wasn't really a circle; this time it was an upward-sloping, narrow piece of ground."

What does the word Surveillance **most likely** mean?

(A) safety

(B) construction

(C) understanding

(D) viewing

Part B: Which sentence from the text **best** supports your answer in part A?

(A) "When they reached the job site, Dad looked around for a spot from which his son could watch the action."

(B) "It was a safe distance away from the area marked out for the foundation."

(C) "Dad knew that construction could be a dangerous business, and he made sure Murphy knew it, too."

(D) "Murphy understood that if he ever ran onto the field near the machines, he would never get to come along again."

22 Read the sentences from the text.

What is similar in Murphy watching the ant farm over breakfast and Murphy watching the workers at the job site?

(A) both show boring activity

(B) both show how excavators work

(C) both show a problem that needs solving

(D) both show how ants can help humans

GO ON →

23 Read the sentences from the text.

"Murphy was on pins and needles trying to figure out what was going on, but he knew better than to leave his post. When a tall man in a hard hat walked out to talk to his dad, Murphy could hear a few words of their conversation: 'solid bedrock' . . . 'find just the right spot' . . . 'expensive!'

What does the use of the phrase "on pins and needles" suggest about Murphy? Select **two** choices.

(A) He wanted to understand why the excavator was not digging.

(B) He was annoyed that the excavator was not digging properly.

(C) He was not surprised because he had predicted this happening.

(D) He felt so excited about the excavation that his hands were tingling.

(E) He felt uncomfortable because the situation was suddenly tense.

(F) His body ached from standing in one spot for so long.

GO ON →

24 The following question has two parts. First, answer part A. Then, answer part B.

Part A: Read the sentence from the text.

"Murphy watched in <u>anticipation</u> as his father started up the excavator and drove toward a marked-out area."

What does the word <u>anticipation</u> mean in this sentence?

(A) great fear

(B) safety

(C) hope

(D) silence

Part B: Which phrase from the text **best** supports your answer in part A?

(A) "moved to"

(B) "looking forward to"

(C) "carefully observed"

(D) "arrived at the right spot"

GO ON →

25 The following question has two parts. First, answer part A. Then, answer part B.

Part A: Read the sentence from the text.

"Should he <u>open up</u> and tell his father that he could understand insects? He decided against it."

What does the idiom "open up" mean?

(A) reveal a secret

(B) act very quickly

(C) proceed very slowly

(D) ask his father's permission

Part B: Which detail from the text **best** supports your answer in part A?

(A) "'How on Earth did you know I should'"

(B) "'That was weird!'"

(C) "Murphy thought hard"

(D) "tell his father that he could communicate"

GO ON →

26 The following question has two parts. First, answer part A. Then, answer part B.

Part A: Which statement **best** expresses the theme of the text?

(A) Construction sites can be dangerous.

(B) Ants and humans are both hard workers.

(C) Solutions can come from unexpected sources.

(D) Parents should always listen to their children.

Part B: Which detail from the text best supports your answer in part A?

(A) "he admired the smooth way they turned around, and the way his dad could open and close the huge shovel from inside his cab."

(B) "Murphy understood that if he ever ran onto the field near the machines, he would never get to come along again."

(C) "Later, Murphy's father asked, 'How on Earth did you know I should approach that spot from a few feet back?'"

(D) "Slowly the bucket rose up, removing the most gigantic rock Murphy had ever seen."

27 The following question has two parts. First, answer part A. Then, answer part B.

Part A: How does Murphy figure out how to solve his father's problem?

(A) An ant communicates with him.

(B) He talks to the man in the hard hat.

(C) He looks carefully at the excavator.

(D) He remembers something from a video.

Part B: Which detail from the text supports your answer to Part A?

(A) "Murphy used to watch it over and over"

(B) "Murphy watched in anticipation as his father started up the excavator"

(C) "could hear a few words of their conversation"

(D) "as if trying to send the boy a message."

GO ON →

28 At what point in the text is it clear that "Ant Farm" is not realistic fiction? Provide a key example of this.

_____

_____

_____

_____

_____

_____

GO ON →

Read the text. Then answer the questions.

Animal Tracks and Burrows

Many wild animals are shy and hard to see. They move quickly and hide in tall grass and leafy trees. They often blend in with their surroundings because of their coloring. However, wildlife biologists have written many books about the signs animals leave. If you learn about these clues, you can become an animal detective. This is a very interesting hobby.

Tracks

The police sometimes look for footprints to help find criminals. Animal detectives look for tracks. Animal tracks show up best in sand, snow, and mud. Each kind of animal has a different footprint. But some groups of animals make tracks that share certain characteristics. One important feature is the number of toes.

Dogs and their close relatives (coyotes, foxes, and wolves) have four toes on their front paws and four toes on their back paws. So do the wild members of the cat family, such as bobcats and mountain lions. Other animals with two sets of four toes are rabbits.

Rodents have four toes in front and an extra, fifth toe on each rear paw. Rodents include rats, mice, squirrels, and chipmunks. Unlike rodents, weasels have five toes in front and in back. So do otters, fishers, and badgers, which are related to weasels. So do raccoons, and so do skunks. (Watch out if you see fresh five-and-five tracks!) Some animals, including deer, have two "toes." They don't look like other animal toes, though. These animals have hard hooves. Each hoof is split in two parts.

If an animal leaves behind a clear track on a muddy riverbank or in a snowy field, it is easy to count the exact number of toe marks. However, a track is often blurred because the animal was moving quickly or because rain or wind erased some of the details. For this reason, a good animal detective memorizes the general shape of a track which might be round, oval, or square.

Animal trackers also know how to interpret the pattern of tracks an animal leaves behind as it moves. The way the animal moves is called its "gait." Some animals walk, while others hop. You can tell which is which by looking at their tracks.

GO ON →

Animal Burrows and Holes

A good animal detective looks for more than tracks. For example, he or she learns to identify the holes of animals that burrow, or dig in the ground for shelter. Important things to check for are the size, shape, and location of the hole. These are all clues to the animal that made it.

Animal Gait Patterns

Walker   Hopper

The eastern mole is a little creature that leaves a pile of dirt over the entrance to its burrow, or shelter. The pile is cone-shaped. The entry into the meadow vole's burrow is a small hole no more than two inches across. It is found in open, grassy fields. The eastern chipmunk's hole is the same size as that of the meadow vole, but there is one big difference. The eastern chipmunk usually digs its burrow near a stone wall.

If you see a 12-inch entrance, the burrow could belong to a woodchuck or a badger. If the burrow is in a wooded area, it is likely home to a woodchuck. The distinctive sign of a mole is not a visible entrance. Rather, it is the tunnel itself. Moles tunnel close to the surface. They raise the soil above the tunnel in a long mound. If the mole tunnel is in a swampy area, it may belong to a funny-looking creature called a star-nosed mole. If it is in a hilly area, it may belong to an eastern mole.

Track Shapes

Track	Shape	Example	Animals
Cross			rodents (mice, rats, squirrels)
Round			mountain lion, bobcat, lynx
Oval			Dog-like animals, such as fox, coyote
Heart			deer
Box			weasel, mink, wolverine, badger, otter

GO ON →

29 The following question has two parts. First, answer part A. Then, answer part B.

Part A: What information in the first paragraph **best** describes the author's point of view?

(A) The author enjoys watching animals' behavior in the wild.

(B) The author thinks finding signs of animals is its own reward.

(C) The author wants to make it easier for the reader to find animals.

(D) The author believes the reader should look for books about animals.

Part B: Which sentence from the text **best** supports your answer in part A?

(A) "Many wild animals are shy and hard to see."

(B) "However, wildlife biologists have written many books about the signs animals leave."

(C) "If you learn about these clues, you can become an animal detective."

(D) "This is a very interesting hobby."

30 Read the sentence from the text.

"For example, he or she learns to identify the holes of animals that burrow, or dig in the ground for shelter."

Which phrase from the sentence explains what burrrow means as it is used in the sentence?

(A) "he or she learns"

(B) "identify the holes"

(C) "dig in the ground"

(D) "for shelter"

GO ON →

31 The following question has two parts. First, answer part A. Then, answer part B.

Part A: Which is the **most likely** reason the author included the Animal Gait Patterns chart in the text?

(A) to provide several examples of how dog and rodent tracks look

(B) to teach readers what kinds of tracks are made by dangerous animals

(C) to help readers understand the information about how animals move

(D) to introduce the topic of using different gaits to identify different tracks

Part B: Which sentence from the text **best** supports your answer in part A?

(A) "Each kind of animal has a different footprint."

(B) "For this reason, a good animal detective memorizes the general shape of a track."

(C) "Rodents have four toes in front and an extra, fifth toe on each rear paw."

(D) "Animal trackers also know how to interpret the pattern of tracks an animal leaves behind as it moves."

32 Draw a line from each animal to the number and placement of toes that appear in their tracks.

| fox | two toes in front, two toes in back |

| deer | four toes in front, four toes in back |

| squirrel | four toes in front, five toes in back |

| fisher | five toes in front, five toes in back |

GO ON →

33 The following question has two parts. First, answer part A. Then, answer part B.

Part A: What is the main idea of the text?

(A) Wild animals are very shy.

(B) Identifying animal tracks can be helpful.

(C) You can identify animals by the signs they leave.

(D) Animals have different numbers of toes on their paws.

Part B: Which sentence from the text **best** supports your answer in part A?

(A) "They move quickly and hide in tall grass and leafy trees."

(B) "The police sometimes look for footprints to help find criminals."

(C) "These are all clues to the animal that made it."

(D) "Other animals with two sets of four toes are rabbits."

GO ON →

Read the directions. Then answer the questions.

34 Which phrase correctly completes the sentence?

I _____ for miles and still have not reached my destination.

(A) was walking

(B) had walked

(C) have walked

(D) will have walked

35 Choose the **two** sentences that do **not** have errors in grammar.

(A) I like either omelets or scrambled eggs for breakfast.

(B) I like neither omelets or scrambled eggs for breakfast.

(C) I like neither omelets nor scrambled eggs for breakfast.

(D) I do not like either omelets nor scrambled eggs for breakfast.

(E) I do not like neither omelets or scrambled eggs for breakfast.

(F) I do not like neither omelets nor scrambled eggs for breakfast.

36 Which word correctly completes the sentence?

If I could find the time, I _____ to play the guitar.

(A) will learn

(B) would learn

(C) have learned

(D) would have learned

GO ON →

37 A student is writing a story for her teacher about an old sailing ship. The student needs to add more exact description to her story. Which word **best** describes what the narrator felt?

That day on the boat, the sky was cloudy and strange. The sea spray felt cold on my face, and the wind was _____. I wanted to go back to my nice cozy home.

The water was becoming choppy and rough. Glassy waves rose up from the water to a height of six or seven feet. I looked at my dad at the wheel and asked, "Are we in trouble?"

(A) refreshing

(B) blowing

(C) cooling

(D) harsh

GO ON →

38 A student is writing a report for her science teacher about exercise on the International Space Station. Read the draft of the report. Then answer the question.

How Astronauts Keep Fit in Space

On the International Space Station (ISS), astronauts experience no gravity. That means they are free to float around, which is a lot of fun but makes it really hard to exercise. Can you imagine doing a pushup and just flying up to the roof? Or jogging when every step launches you into the air?

This is a problem for astronauts who stay on the ISS for months. If astronauts did not use their muscles at all, they would not be able to walk when they got back to Earth. So how do they keep fit? They use special equipment.

The most important piece of equipment is the Treadmill Vibration Machine. This machine has a harness that pulls astronauts against a treadmill, like gravity. However, without gravity, walking is not a good exercise. To fix this, the machine shakes the harness to work the muscles and make exercise harder.

The writer wants to make her meaning more clear. Which phrase **best** replaces the underlined phrase in the text?

(A) walking only works leg muscles

(B) lifting legs up and down is too easy

(C) lifting legs up and down is dangerous

(D) walking does not increase fitness levels

GO ON →

39 A student is writing a report about ancient civilizations for his social studies teacher. Read the draft of his introduction. Then answer the question.

There were many ancient civilizations, like Greece and China. They all were different. Sometimes, these differences were caused by social things, like language. Other times, these differences were caused by <u>real</u> things, like geography. For example, Greece has many mountains and islands. This made cities develop without central control. In China, early people settled along the same river. They needed a large government to control the river's floods.

The writer wants to make his meaning more clear. Which word **best** replaces the underlined word in the text?

(A) important

(B) known

(C) regular

(D) physical

SESSION 1

Read the text. Then answer the questions.

Speaking the Same Language

On the first day of school, I noticed a new girl sitting in the front row in class. She was wearing a navy blue skirt and a white, button-down shirt, and her hair was in long braids tied with ribbons.

The teacher welcomed us and then announced, "Class, this is Fiona; she just moved here from Great Britain. I am sure you will be especially welcoming, and help her with any questions she may have about school."

When the bell rang for lunch, everyone started to rush out the door. The new girl looked a little lost, so I decided to go out on a limb and introduce myself. (This was a little bit out of character for me because I usually wait for other people to talk to me first.) I said, "Hi, my name is Nina. I absolutely love your braids!"

"My what?" asked the new girl. "You know, your braids," I repeated. I could feel myself blushing and started to wish I hadn't spoken up at all.

"Oh," the girl laughed, "you must mean my plaits—that's what we call them back home in England. I'm sorry, I feel as if I speak a completely different language sometimes. May I sit with you in the canteen today?"

Now it was my turn to be completely baffled. I thought a canteen was a metal container used for carrying water on a hike. How could you possibly sit in one, and why on Earth would you want to?

"She means the cafeteria," piped up my bossy friend, Audrey. She joined us as we walked down the crowded hallway. "My mom is from England. We go there every summer to visit my relatives, so I can help translate."

"Brilliant!" exclaimed Fiona.

I have to admit that Audrey was very helpful in the lunch line. First, Fiona asked the server for extra *courgettes*. Audrey quickly said, "She means zucchini." Then Fiona asked if the *biscuits* had any nuts in them. Audrey translated, "cookies."

"Goodness," sighed Fiona when they sat down with their trays and started eating. "That was exhausting. How am I supposed to remember all of these new words? I'll probably get confused, and then the lunch servers will think I'm completely *daft*!"

GO ON →

"Senseless?" I guessed. Both Fiona and Audrey nodded! It seemed like I was finally catching on.

Over lunch, we all got to know each other. I really liked Fiona, but sometimes I felt a little left out. Once she said she forgot to take a serviette (a napkin). Then she wished she had some clingfilm (plastic wrap) so she could wrap up her cookie for a snack. Audrey nodded, clearly understanding what these British English terms referred to, while I had no idea.

At the end of the school day, we all rode home on the same bus. Fiona plopped down into a seat next to Audrey. I was going to take a seat behind them, but Fiona must have noticed my disappointed expression, and she squeezed in to make room for me, as well.

Fiona started looking at a flyer about after-school activities that Ms. Lopez had handed out at the end of the day. After quickly running her finger down the list, Fiona frowned.

"I'm so disappointed that there's no football!"

I began to explain that football was more of a high school sport in the United States. Then Audrey interrupted. "She means soccer, Nina."

I just couldn't take it anymore! I was the one who had worked up the courage to approach the new girl first to try to make her feel comfortable and welcomed, but now Audrey was taking over.

"Stop acting like such a know-it-all, Audrey!" I burst out. "Just because you go to England every summer doesn't mean you know everything about everything!"

Audrey looked shocked. She was quiet for a minute, but then she said, "I'm sorry, Nina, I don't mean to act like a know-it-all. Actually, I don't understand a lot of the things Fiona says. Like, what did you mean when you said you like my *trainers*, Fiona?"

Fiona just giggled and pointed down at Audrey's shoes.

"I have an idea," Fiona said. "The three of us can work together to make a British-American dictionary. It will give translations of all the terms that are different between the two forms of English. I can use it to learn American English. You two can use it if you want to speak my brand of British English when we're having conversations. Can you both come over to my house this weekend to get started?"

Audrey and I looked at each other for a second, and then nodded and smiled as we looked back at Fiona.

"Genius!" said an excited Fiona.

GO ON →

1 The following question has two parts. First, answer part A. Then, answer part B.

Part A: Read the paragraphs from the text.

"Oh, the girl laughed, 'you must mean my plaits--that's what we call them back home in England. I'm sorry, I feel as if I speak a completely different language sometimes. May I sit with you in the canteen today?"

Now it was my turn to be completely <u>baffled</u>. I thought a canteen was a metal container used for carrying water on a hike. How could you possibly sit in one, and why on Earth would you want to?

What does the word <u>baffled</u> **most likely** mean?

(A) certain

(B) confused

(C) mad

(D) shy

Part B: Which detail from the text **best** supports your answer in part A?

(A) "'started to wish I hadn't spoken up at all.'"

(B) "'that's what we call them back home in England.'"

(C) "'I'm sorry'"

(D) "'How could you possibly sit in one'"

GO ON →

2 The following question has two parts. First, answer part A. Then, answer part B.

Part A: Which statement **best** describes the relationship between Nina and Audrey after Fiona first arrives at the school?

(A) Nina feels Audrey is acting like a know-it-all.

(B) Nina and Audrey always help each other through problems.

(C) Audrey helps Nina by telling her what Fiona is talking about.

(D) Audrey and Nina both begin to understand what Fiona is saying.

Part B: Which sentence from the text **best** supports your answer in part A?

(A) "'She means the cafeteria,' piped up my bossy friend, Audrey."

(B) "I have to admit that Audrey was very helpful in the lunch line."

(C) "Then Fiona asked if the biscuits had any nuts in them. Audrey translated, 'cookies.'"

(D) "'Senseless?' I guessed. Both Fiona and Audrey nodded! I was catching on."

GO ON →

3 Match each conclusion about the narrator's point of view with the sentence from the text that supports it.

Nina is anxious about being Fiona's friend.

Fiona is concerned about the feelings of others.

Nina has a difficult time expressing herself.

She squeezed in to make room for me, too."

"I'm sorry, I feel as if I speak a completely different language sometimes."

I really liked Fiona, but sometimes I felt a little left out.

At the end of the school day, we all rode home on the same bus.

The new girl, however, looked a little lost, so I decided to go out on a limb and introduce myself.

4 Based on Nina's comments, which statement best describes Audrey's actions at the end of the text?

(A) Audrey will stop talking to Nina.

(B) Audrey will choose to write the book herself.

(C) Audrey will keep interrupting Nina and Fiona.

(D) Audrey will include everyone in the conversation.

GO ON →

5 Summarize the theme of the text. Use key details from the text to support your summary.

_____

_____

_____

_____

_____

_____

GO ON →

Read the text. Then answer the questions.

A Remarkable Scientist

During World War I in France (1914–1918), many soldiers died because they did not get good medical care. Doctors at the time did not know about many procedures and medicines that could have saved lives. It was also very hard to get the best medical equipment to the areas where soldiers were wounded. However, that situation began to change. A brand-new medical technique called the X ray was invented, and a scientist was able to bring the invention to the battlefield. Today, the X ray is still the primary tool that doctors use to find broken bones and other health problems.

Marie Curie was 47 years old at the time. She was a famous scientist who had been sent away from Paris for her own protection during the war. But she realized that the research she was doing at the time could help save lives—and she kept at it.

First, she persuaded some automakers to turn some cars into vans so she could carry X ray equipment in them. They agreed. Then she trained her 17-year-old daughter Irene to use the new equipment and brought her along. They lived the hard life of soldiers near the fighting and trained others to do the same work.

Their X ray vans were easy to recognize and decorated with a red cross. The vans were so familiar to soldiers that they began to call them petites Curies, or "little Curies." By the end of the war, Marie and her daughter had developed over 200 X ray units. They had supervised over a million X rays.

Helping an Adopted Country

One thing that made her work so special to the people of France was that Marie Curie had been born and raised in the city of Warsaw in Poland. Her parents were teachers, and she had been an outstanding student her entire life. Much of Poland was controlled by Russia at the time, and she and her father supported a movement to free the country from Russia. She soon realized that to get a full education in the sciences, she would have to leave her home country. Poland at the time did not admit female students to institutes of higher learning.

First, Marie worked to support her older sister, who moved to Paris to get medical training. Then her sister did the same for Marie when Marie came to study physics in Paris in 1891. Marie had just enough money to pay for college, a tiny attic apartment, and very little food. Even though she was often sick during this period, she completed her work in only three years.

Because Marie was a top student, she got a scholarship to continue her work. Soon after that, the world sat up and took notice. In 1894, Marie began to do research in

GO ON →

a small lab run by Pierre Curie. They married the next year and began to work together on research. Marie persuaded Pierre to help her finish the work required to get the highest degree in physics. She became the first woman in the world to earn a doctor's degree in science.

Rising Stars

Once Marie and Pierre married, their work grew and their fame took off. Marie convinced Pierre they should work on a new discovery by German and French scientists. They had discovered that some substances gave off rays that could pass through wood or human skin. Marie was the first to call this *radioactivity*.

Soon, the Curies discovered a new element that was radioactive. Marie named it *polonium* to honor the country of Poland where she grew up. After discovering another new radioactive element, they were awarded the Nobel Prize in Physics in 1903. The Nobel Prize is the highest award in the world for scientific discoveries. Pierre was given a good teaching job at the best college in France. Marie was able to do research in a good laboratory. They had two daughters, and Pierre's father helped care for them.

A Sudden Turn

In 1906, Pierre Curie stepped off a curb on a rainy night in Paris directly in front of a wagon pulled by horses. He was immediately trampled to death. Not long afterward, Pierre's father became sick and died also.

Marie's world was suddenly turned upside down, but she continued her work. She was so successful that she was awarded a second Nobel Prize, this time in chemistry. She was the first person to receive two Nobel Prizes. She is still the only person in history to receive them in two different sciences.

Deadly Effects

The Curies' research paved the way for many later discoveries. But what the Curies did not realize at the time was that radioactive substances can be very harmful. They handled radioactive materials without any protection.

The materials were fascinating. They gave off a faint, blue glow and were actually warm to the touch. Marie Curie was exposed to their harmful rays for many years before people realized their danger. Because she absorbed so much radioactivity, even the objects around her were affected. Today, her cookbook has to be stored in a protective case so that people are not harmed by the radioactivity.

Marie Curie died in 1934 from the effects of harmful radiation. During World War I, she had written, "I am resolved to put all my strength at the service of my adopted country." She had put all of her strength into gaining scientific knowledge as well. She remains one of the most respected and honored scientists in history.

GO ON →

6 The author organized the first section of the text by describing how Marie Curie helped to save the lives of wounded soldiers . Which details from the text **best** support this structure?

(A) "many soldiers died because they did not get good medical care"

(B) "However, that situation began to change."

(C) "Marie Curie was 47 years old at the time."

(D) "Their X ray vans were easy to recognize and decorated with a red cross."

(E) "They lived the hard life of soldiers near the fighting . . ."

(F) "Marie and her daughter had developed over 200 X ray units."

7 The following question has two parts. First, answer part A. Then, answer part B.

Part A: Read the sentence from the text.

Today, the X ray is still the primary tool that doctors use to find broken bones and other health problems.

What does the word primary **most likely** mean?

(A) latest

(B) safest

(C) most used

(D) least expensive

Part B: Which sentence from the text **best** support your answer in part A?

(A) "But she realized that the research she was doing at the time could help save lives—and she kept at it."

(B) "First, she persuaded some automakers to turn some cars into vans so she could carry X ray equipment in them."

(C) "The vans were so familiar to soldiers that they began to call them petites Curies, or 'little Curies.'"

(D) "They had supervised over a million x-rays."

GO ON →

8 The following question has two parts. First, answer part A. Then, answer part B.

Part A: Read the paragraph from the text.

First, she <u>persuaded</u> some automakers to turn some cars into vans so she could carry X ray equipment in them. They agreed. Then she trained her 17-year-old daughter Irene to use the new equipment and brought her along. They lived the hard life of soldiers near the fighting and trained others to do the same work.

Which word **best** states the meaning of <u>persuaded</u>?

(A) convinced

(B) forced

(C) prevented

(D) tricked

Part B: Which phrase from the text **best** supports your answer in part A?

(A) carry X ray equipment

(B) They agreed . . .

(C) brought her along

(D) lived the hard life of soldiers

GO ON →

9 The following question has two parts. First, answer part A. Then, answer part B.

Part A: Why was information about Marie and Pierre Curie's life together included in the text?

(A) to illustrate Marie's interest in radioactivity

(B) to compare Marie's career to that of her husband

(C) to contrast Marie's adopted country to her homeland

(D) to describe Marie's rise to fame in the world of science

Part B: Which detail from the text **best** supports your answer in part A?

(A) "Marie convinced Pierre they should work on a new discovery by German and French scientists."

(B) "Marie named it polonium to honor the country of Poland where she grew up."

(C) "After discovering another new radioactive element, they were awarded the Nobel Prize in Physics in 1903."

(D) "They had two daughters, and Pierre's father helped care for them."

10 Which sentence from the test **best** supports the author's conclusion that Marie Curie was loyal to France?

(A) "The vans were so familiar to soldiers that they began to call them petites Curies, or 'little Curies.'"

(B) "One thing that made her work so special to the people of France was that Marie Curie had been born and raised in the city of Warsaw in Poland."

(C) "Then her sister did the same for Marie when Marie came to study physics in Paris in 1891."

(D) "During World War I, she had written, "I am resolved to put all my strength at the service of my adopted country."

GO ON →

11 The following question has two parts. First, answer part A. Then, answer part B.

Part A: According to the article, what was the cause of Marie Curie's death?

(A) not wearing proper protection while working with radioactive materials

(B) sadness over the death of Pierre Curie and his father

(C) exhaustion from many years of hard work as a research scientist

(D) living like a soldier during World War I

Part B: Which detail from the text **best** supports your answer in Part A?

(A) "They lived the hard life of soldiers near the fighting . . ."

(B) "Not long afterward, Pierre's father became sick and died also."

(C) "She became the first woman in the world to earn a doctor's degree in science."

(D) "They handled radioactive materials without any protection."

GO ON →

12 The following question has two parts. First, answer part A. Then, answer part B.

Part A: What conclusion about Marie Curie is supported by the text?

(A) Marie's research helped to created change in the future.

(B) Marie's scientific work was more important than Pierre's.

(C) The loss of Marie's husband Pierre did not impact her work.

(D) Marie used her fame to protect her family from wartime danger.

Part B: Which detail from the text **best** supports your answer in part A?

(A) "She was a famous scientist who had been sent away from Paris for her own protection during the war.

(B) "Because Marie was a top student, she got a scholarship to continue her work.

(C) "She was so successful that she was awarded a second Nobel Prize, this time in chemistry."

(D) "The Curies' research paved the way for many later discoveries."

13 Draw a line from each idea to the detail from the text that supports it.

Marie Curie was determined to succeed even when facing hardships.

Scientific discoveries can have a positive impact on the lives of others.

Even though she was often sick during this period, she completed her work in only three years.

Because she absorbed so much radioactivity, even the objects around her were affected.

In 1894, Marie began to do research in a small lab run by Pierre Curie.

A brand-new medical technique called the X ray was invented, and a scientist was able to bring the invention to the battlefield.

Today, her cookbook has to be stored in a protective case so that people are not harmed by the radioactivity.

GO ON →

Read the directions. Then answer the questions.

14 A student is writing a research report about pets. She wrote an opinion in the report. Read the opinion. Then answer the question.

The best small pet for a busy child is a hamster.

The student took notes about hamsters. Which notes **best** support the student's opinion. Select **two** options.

(A) Hamsters love exercise.

(B) Hamsters are easy to care for.

(C) Hamsters sleep during the day.

(D) Hamsters are very common pets.

(E) Hamsters are very healthy animals.

(F) Hamsters can move around inside a ball.

15 A student made a plan for a research report. Read the plan. Then answer the directions.

Research Report Plan

Topic: Old-Time Carousels
Audience: classmates
Purpose: to inform
Research Question: What is the value of old-time carousels?

The student found information for the research report. Which sentences **best** answer the research question? Select **two** options.

(A) Carousels remind people of the past.

(B) Many people fix old carousels as a hobby.

(C) Hand-carved carousel horses are expensive works of art.

(D) The most beautiful carousels were built by the Dentzel Company.

(E) The modern carousel or merry-go-round is a mid-19th century invention.

(F) Dentzel horses sell on online auction sites for thousands of dollars.

GO ON →

16 A student is writing a report about modern bridge design. The student found the following sources. Which source would most likely contain information for the report?

(A) a website about building bridges

(B) a magazine article about famous bridges

(C) a book called *Early Bridges*

(D) a novel titled *The Bridge Over the River of Life*

17 A student has made a plan for research. Read the plan and the directions that follow.

Research Report Plan
Topic: Healthy Lunch Options
Audience: fellow students
Purpose: to inform
Research Question: Is the average school lunch good for you?

The student found the following sources. Which source would **most likely** have information for the report?

(A) a website about healthy eating habits

(B) a diagram explaining the food pyramid

(C) a lunch menu from the school cafeteria

(D) a recipe for making a sugar-free dessert

GO ON →

18 A student is writing a letter to the principal about allowing the fifth grade class to bike to school. Read the draft of the letter. Then complete the task that follows.

Dear Principal Wiggins,

Please consider letting fifth graders bike to and from school. We are old enough to ride our bicycles this distance, and we would appreciate having this special privilege and responsibility. There are many benefits to kids riding their bikes to and from school. It would save gas in our buses and this money could go toward hiring a crossing guard. Riding bikes is also great exercise and would help students feel more focused and energetic in class. I know safety is a concern, but some parents have volunteered to ride with us. Also, there are sidewalks and crosswalks in this area.

Based on information in the student's draft, write a paragraph that concludes the letter supporting the student's argument for biking to school.

_____

_____

_____

_____

_____

19 A student is writing a narrative for class about something that made him proud. The student wants to revise the draft to include dialogue. Read the draft of the narrative and answer the question that follows.

Something that made me feel proud was teaching my five-year-old brother how to read. Caleb always liked to be read to and to look at storybooks together. He would watch me reading big chapter books for homework and ask me what they were about. One day he said he wanted to learn how to read, too. So I got some pens and paper and we started with the alphabet. I taught him what sound each letter makes. Then we moved on to small words. <u>Finally, I helped him sound out his name. You should have seen how excited he was!</u>

The writer wants to add dialogue to the narrative. Which of the following sentences **best** replaces the underlined text?

Ⓐ "Sound out this word," I said. "Caleb," he read. "Wow, I'm excited!"

Ⓑ I said, "Let's read this word now." Caleb read his name and got excited. "I did it! I read my name."

Ⓒ "Now I am going to help you sound out this word," I said. He read out loud, "Caleb. That is my name! Now I can read my name."

Ⓓ I tapped the letters and said, "Now try this one: C-A-L-E-B. Sound it out, buddy." He worked it out slowly, "Kuh ... kah ... Kay-leb. Caleb. Hey, I read my name!"

20 A student is writing a report about Mark Twain. The student wants to revise the draft to better link ideas. Read the draft of the report and complete the task that follows.

Mark Twain was a famous American author who lived from 1835 to 1910. He grew up in Hannibal, Missouri, and his books helped readers imagine what it was like to be a boy in the South. In 1876, he wrote *The Adventures of Tom Sawyer*, and it was very popular. Its sequel, *The Adventures of Huckleberry Finn,* was an even greater success. It has been called the "great American novel." Twain wrote many other novels, essays, and short stories in his lifetime.

Choose the **best** word or phrase to connect the underlined sentences.

(A) In fact,

(B) However,

(C) Above all,

(D) Meanwhile,

SESSION 2

Read the text. Then answer the questions.

Staying in Touch

As Abby approached the front door of the nursing home, she felt very beaten down. When she had started volunteering a few months ago, she had had high hopes. She had remembered her grandmother before she died and thought about how important it had been to her every time Abby visited. It was hard to find the time, but now she came two mornings a week when she did not have classes at the university.

Lately, it had been harder, because she felt she was not making much of a difference to anyone. She moved patients around by pushing their wheelchairs and helped out during lunch, and sometimes she led the exercise class, chanting "One, two, one, two," slowly to the music as a small group seated in chairs or wheelchairs raised their arms above their heads.

However, she put on a happy face and greeted Nathan, who always sat by the door. Later, she went to the community room to take her 15-minute break and opened her phone to check for voice or text messages. Then she checked her social media sites to see what was happening with her friends and family, and was totally focused on a message from her brother when Greta rolled her wheelchair almost on top of her.

"What are you doing?" Greta demanded. She was always a little pushy, but Abby liked her. Abby wondered sometimes if Greta was loud just to make sure people would listen to her.

"Checking up on my brother," said Abby. "He's doing some sort of research project in New Zealand."

"You can tell all that just from that little thing in your hand?" She shook her head; it was hard for her to comprehend.

"Sure, I get to read whatever he feels like writing, he answers questions I send him, and he can send me pictures, too, even movies."

"I wish I could do that," said Greta, "but you can't teach an old dog new tricks." Abby sensed a little sadness in her voice.

"Whom would you check up on?"

GO ON →

Greta looked out the window for a moment as she thought about how to answer, and finally turned toward Abby. "My children are wonderful," she said, "but they're too far away. One son is on the East Coast, one's on the West Coast, and my little girl is in Texas."

She caught herself and added, "She's not really a little girl, though, since she turned 33 last month."

"How often do you hear from them?"

"They come to visit, but only about once a year. We tried to make a schedule to talk on the phone, but the time difference makes it so we can only talk really early in the morning before I'm awake, or late at night when I'm already asleep. It's hard . . . ." Her voice trailed off, and she turned her wheelchair away from Abby.

Before she left that day, Abby stopped in to see her supervisor, Mrs. Hanson. "What do you think about getting a computer for the community room?" asked Abby.

"A computer? What for?"

"So the residents could e-mail their relatives."

"E-mail? Most of them hardly use the telephone; they'd be afraid to use a computer."

"I'm not sure that's true. I think there are a few who would love it."

Mrs. Hanson frowned and looked unsure, remaining silent for a long while. Finally, she said, "You've got a laptop, so why don't you see if you can get some of them interested in using your computer? If there's enough interest, we could try to get a computer for everyone to use."

On her next day at the home, Abby put up signs:

> Computer Class 10:00 P.M., Thursday: Learning to use e-mail addresses.

That first Thursday, Abby found Greta and her friend Susan waiting for her. As Abby opened up her laptop, Susan blurted out, "I only came because Greta made me!"

"Stop being a baby," growled Greta. "You're always talking about staying in touch with your grandkids. Abby's going to teach us how."

Abby set her laptop on a table and slowly walked them through setting up an e-mail account. They followed along, but when it was Greta's turn to enter information, she began rubbing her twisted fingers, explaining, "My fingers just don't work very well anymore."

GO ON →

Abby moved to her side and gave her a pencil with the eraser end down. "Here, use this. It will work just as well."

Greta soon created an account and sent several short e-mail messages. Susan watched Greta like a hawk and then did the same, although she used her fingers to type. To their surprise, each of them received a response within a few minutes.

The next Thursday, Greta and Susan were waiting at the front of a line with two other women and a man leaning against the wall.

The week after that, the line stretched down the hall.

During that morning session, Mrs. Hanson interrupted Abby as she taught another resident the basics. "Our community computer is coming next week, but it looks like we'll have to make some rules about time limits. So many residents will want to use it!"

Abby just smiled. For Greta, Susan, and many of the others, e-mail was just the beginning. Wait until they hit the senior chat rooms and social media sites, she thought. There was a whole new world waiting for them.

GO ON →

21 The following question has two parts. First, answer part A. Then, answer part B.

Part A: What does the adage, "you can't teach an old dog new tricks" suggest about how Greta is feeling?

(A) She is lonely.

(B) She is tired.

(C) She is hopeful.

(D) She is disappointed.

Part B: Which detail from the text **best** supports your answer in part A?

(A) "she had had high hopes"

(B) "Abby sensed a little sadness in her voice."

(C) "she was not making much of a difference"

(D) "'Whom would you check up on?'"

22 The following question has two parts. First, answer part A. Then, answer part B.

Part A: What does Mrs. Hanson think will happen if they get a computer for the residents?

(A) few residents have relatives to contact

(B) many residents would not want to use it

(C) some residents would not share it with others

(D) many residents would complain about the cost of buying one.

Part B: Which detail from the text **best** supports your answer in part A?

(A) "'They come to visit, but only about once a year.'"

(B) "'they'd be afraid to use a computer'"

(C) "'we could try to get a computer for everyone to use.'"

(D) "'we'll have to make some rules about time limits.'"

GO ON →

23 The following question has two parts. First, answer part A. Then, answer part B.

Part A: Read the sentences from the text.

"'Stop being a baby,' <u>growled</u> Greta. 'You're always talking about staying in touch with your grandkids. Abby's going to teach us how.'"

What effect does the author create by using the word <u>growled</u>?

(A) Greta is unhappy and dislikes people.

(B) Greta sounds like she has a sore throat.

(C) Greta is sad that she can't get what she wants.

(D) Greta speaks gruffly to others.

Part B: Which detail from the text **best** supports your answer in part A?

(A) "She was always a little pushy, but Abby liked her."

(B) "Abby wondered sometimes if Greta was loud just to make sure people would listen to her."

(C) "That first Thursday, Abby found Greta and her friend Susan waiting for her."

(D) "As Abby opened up her laptop, Susan blurted out, 'I only came because Greta made me!'"

GO ON →

24 Based on what you have read, what will Abby **most likely** do next?

(A) encourage family members to visit more often

(B) quit going to college so she can work at the nursing home

(C) teach the nursing home residents more about using computers

(D) stop volunteering at the nursing home and spend more time with her family

(E) visit New Zealand to see her brother

(F) make rules about the amount of time for computer use

25 The following question has two parts. First, answer part A. Then, answer part B.

Part A: Which statement **best** identifies the theme of the text?

(A) Ongoing learning is a difficult activity for seniors.

(B) Internet use can improve the quality of life for seniors.

(C) Volunteers make a big difference in the lives of others.

(D) It takes a pushy person to change the habits of others.

Part B: Which detail from the text **best** supports your answer in part A?

(A) "Lately, it had been harder, because she felt she was not making much of a difference to anyone."

(B) "'I think there are a few who would love it.'"

(C) "'Stop being a baby,' growled Greta."

(D) "There was a whole new world waiting for them."

GO ON →

26 Which of the statements would the narrator most likely agree with? Choose **two** options.

(A) Seniors would rather write letters than type e-mails.

(B) It is important for nursing homes to provide a wide range of activities.

(C) Seniors have a lot more interests than people might guess.

(D) People often find it challenging to stay in touch with one another.

(E) Young volunteers find that helping seniors is difficult.

(F) New technology is useful to people of all ages.

27 Complete the chart by indicating which characteristics describe Abby and Greta. Some characteristics describe both.

Characteristics	Abby	Greta
discouraged	☐	☐
determined to help others	☐	☐
misses someone close to them	☐	☐
confused by new technology	☐	☐
creates change	☐	☐
persuades someone to try something new	☐	☐

GO ON →

28 What conclusions can be drawn about how Abby overcame her feelings of being "beaten down"? Support your answer with details from the text.

_____

_____

_____

_____

_____

GO ON →

Read the text. Then answer the questions.

Fighting the War at Home

World War II affected the lives of nearly all Americans. About one of every eight people served in the military, a total of more than 16 million men and women. More than a million were killed or wounded.

However, not everyone could join the army or navy. Many people could not serve because they were too old or too young. Some had physical problems. Women and African Americans faced other obstacles, such as unfair treatment, that prevented them from joining. Perhaps most important, American workers were needed at home. They had to produce the guns, ammunition, clothing, food, and other supplies to fight the war.

Life was very hard for most of the soldiers. But life at home was a challenge, too. All Americans were asked to make sacrifices so the troops could have what they needed to win the war.

Rationing

When World War II began, the United States was just beginning to recover from the Great Depression. Its farms and factories were not producing at the highest levels. Production had to increase rapidly to equip and feed a large military force stationed overseas. Until production increased, the American people had to use less of many products so more could go to the military.

The federal government met this problem by beginning a rationing program. Rationing means allowing each person to buy or use only a certain amount of something. When there was a shortage of a certain product, the government temporarily controlled how much each person could buy. At different times, rubber tires, gasoline, heating oil, shoes, and many types of foods were rationed.

One of the first things rationed was rubber. The Japanese had taken over many rubber plantations in Asia. The United States did not have a supply of raw materials to make rubber. The government asked people to turn in all old automobile and bicycle tires. They couldn't buy more unless they could show a very important need.

For most of the war, people had to use one of the 8,000 ration boards, or offices, that sprouted up around the country. Before they could buy rationed goods, each household had to get a book or coupons or tokens for them. Then they used their ration books to buy the amount the government decided was reasonable for a certain period of time. Even if a family had plenty of money, they could not buy an extra pound of cheese every month. Wealthy families could not buy more shoes than other families.

GO ON →

Most families had to plan their meals carefully to use only the amount that was allowed. At the time, women did most of the shopping, and they studied their ration books carefully before they went to the store. Men tended to do most of the driving and had to carry their gasoline rations with them each time they needed to fill up. Many people treated their ration books like gold.

The government even controlled women's clothing to force conservation of products needed by the military. For example, skirts were made with hems that were turned under at the bottom. It was a part of the skirt that was not seen. The government reduced wasted cloth by stating that the hems could not be more than two inches wide. They limited the width of women's leather belts to two inches as well.

Victory Gardens

American farmers could not supply enough food at the beginning of the war. They needed to feed people at home as well as the military and America's allies. The U.S. government encouraged people to plant small vegetable gardens wherever there were good spots. Many people turned their lawns into gardens. In this way, they were able to eat fresh vegetables that were not available at the stores. Many cities and towns let people plant gardens in park areas.

The U.S. government established the Office of War Information to support rationing, small gardens, and other programs. This office published news articles, posters, and short movies to show how important it was for people at home to support the war. To feel good about gardening, people named the small gardens "Victory Gardens." By planting gardens, Americans were helping their troops achieve victory.

Shared Sacrifice

When the war was over, Americans were happy to return to a life without rationing, Victory Gardens, or any of the other sacrifices they had to make.

On the other hand, many people had some fond memories of the sacrifices they made during the war. It felt good for everyone to work together. People were not always as comfortable as they would have liked. However, they at home were helping to fight the war, and they felt a part of the victory in the end.

Wartime Rationing (1942–1945)	
Rationed Items	**Rationing Period**
Tires	January 1942–December 1945
Gasoline	May 1942–August 1945
Shoes	February 1943–October 1945
Sugar	May 1942–December 1947
Coffee	November 1942–July 1943
Cheese	March 1943–November 1945
Meat	March 1943–November 1945

GO ON →

29 The following question has two parts. First, answer part A. Then, answer part B.

Part A: What is **most likely** the author's intent by mentioning the number of Americans who served in the military in the opening paragraph?

(A) The author wanted to show that the war affected most Americans.

(B) The author wanted to present the idea that war involves a select few.

(C) The author wanted to use facts to inform readers about wartime struggles.

(D) The author wanted to present the idea that most Americans were in the military.

Part B: Which sentence from the text **best** supports your answer in part A?

(A) "Life was very hard for most of the soldiers."

(B) "All Americans were asked to make sacrifices so the troops could have what they needed to win the war."

(C) "When World War II began, the United States was just beginning to recover from the Great Depression."

(D) "The Japanese had taken over many rubber plantations in Asia."

GO ON →

30 The following question has two parts. First, answer part A. Then, answer part B.

Part A: Read the sentence from the text.

Women and African Americans faced other <u>obstacles</u>, such as unfair treatment, that prevented them from joining.

What does the word <u>obstacles</u> **most likely** mean?

(A) actions

(B) problems

(C) stages

(D) steps

Part B: Which phrase from the text **best** supports your answer in part A?

(A) "were needed at home"

(B) "prevented them"

(C) "Perhaps most important"

(D) "They had to produce"

GO ON →

31 Read this sentence from the text.

However, they at home were helping to fight the war, and they felt a part of the victory in the end.

Which details from the text support the idea that Americans at home helped their troops win the war? Select **all** that apply.

(A) "About one of every eight people served in the military"

(B) "The government asked people to turn in all old automobile and bicycle tires."

(C) "Even if a family had plenty of money, they could not buy an extra pound of cheese every month."

(D) "In this way they were able to eat fresh vegetables that were not available at the stores."

(E) "Many people turned their lawns into gardens."

(F) "The U.S. government established the Office of War Information"

GO ON →

32 Which inference can be made about the author's opinion of rationing?

(A) Rationing was forced on the people so all citizens could feel like they were part of the war effort.

(B) Rationing was needed because the United States did not have enough materials to fight the war.

(C) Rationing was not necessary when the war began but was needed later as the war dragged on for years.

(D) Rationing was never supported by Americans but was a requirement in order to supply the army and navy.

33 Which of the statements is supported by both the text and the chart?

(A) Rationing started before the war began.

(B) Rationing for all products was only temporary.

(C) Rationing was not really necessary to win the war.

(D) Rationing covered nearly everything people bought.

GO ON →

Name: _____   Date: _____

Read the directions. Then answer the question.

 34 The sentence below contains one error in grammar usage. Read the sentence. Then answer the question.

If I could learn to play the guitar, I will be the greatest rock star of all time.

Which **two** versions of the sentence have been correctly edited for grammar usage?

(A) If I could play the guitar, I should be the greatest rock star of all time.

(B) If I will learn to play the guitar, I will be the greatest rock star of all time.

(C) When I learn to play the guitar, I will be the greatest rock star of all time.

(D) When I learned to play the guitar, I will be the greatest rock star of all time.

(E) When I learn to play the guitar, I would be the greatest rock star of all time.

(F) If I could learn to play the guitar, I would be the greatest rock star of all time.

35 Select the phrase that correctly completes the paragraph.

Ms. Sorrentino had a busy day planned. She needed to work through lunch to finish her website. Before lunch, she called her friend and said, "I __ able to go to the restaurant."

(A) will not be

(B) would not be

(C) had not been

(D) should not be

GO ON →

36 Choose the conjunction that **best** shows that the two games happened at different times.

The Pirates played the Bears _____ the Knights played the Raiders.

(A) so

(B) after

(C) as long as

(D) in order that

37 A student is writing a journal entry about his day for English class. Read the draft of the entry. Then answer the question.

My uncle came to dinner tonight. He is a member of the fire department rescue squad, and always has interesting stories. Last week he was called to a factory. A pipe had burst and some workers got hit with really bad steam. They had burns and were in a lot of pain when he showed up, but he was able to take care of them.

The writer wants to replace the phrase really bad to make his meaning more clear. Which phrases would make his word choice **better**? Select **two** choices.

(A) very terrible

(B) pretty warm

(C) fast rushing

(D) blistering hot

(E) really frightening

(F) high temperature

GO ON →

38 A student is writing a report about women's voting rights for her teacher. Read the draft of the report and answer the question that follows.

Women could not vote in most states a century ago. To change this, many activists gathered in public places across America for nonviolent <u>fights</u> against injustice.

Which more exact word **best** replaces <u>fights</u>?

(A) attacks

(B) battles

(C) gathers

(D) protests

39 A student is writing a report about civil responsibilities for social studies class. Read the draft of the report and answer the question that follows.

The United States Congress is elected. It is the duty of <u>people</u> to vote in every election. That is the primary way that they can make their opinions known to their representatives.

Which more exact word **best** replaces the <u>people</u>?

(A) adults

(B) countrymen

(C) citizens

(D) everyone

Narrative Performance Task

Task:

Your class has been learning about nature and living in the wilderness. Now, you are going to create a magazine to share what you have learned. Each student will write something for the magazine.

Before you decide what you will write about nature and the wilderness, you do some research. As part of your research, you have uncovered the following three sources that discuss wilderness education programs, farming in the city, and how to survive in the wilderness. After you have reviewed these sources, you will answer some questions about them. Briefly scan the sources and the three questions that follow. Then, go back and review the sources carefully to gather the information you will need to answer the questions and write your narrative story for the class magazine.

In Part 2, you will write a story using details from the three sources.

Directions for Part 1:

You will now look at three sources. You can look at any of the sources as often as you like.

Research Questions:

After looking at the sources, use the rest of the time in Part 1 to answer three questions about them. Your answers to these questions will be scored. Also, your answers will help you think about the information you have read, which should help you write your narrative story. You may refer to the sources when you think it would be helpful. You may also look at your notes.

GO ON →

Source #1: From the City to the Wilderness

People are part of the natural world. We depend upon natural resources such as sunlight, water, and food to survive, and we share the planet with animals, birds, and insects. We are affected by the weather and by natural disasters, such as earthquakes and floods.

Human beings also have an impact on the natural world. We cut down forests, change the direction of rivers, dig gold and drill oil out of the earth, and throw away mountains of trash. Our actions can help or hurt nature.

Long ago, most people lived close to nature. They hunted and farmed for their food. They knew which plants they could use for medicines when they got sick. When they took long journeys, they used the stars overhead to tell their direction. Ancient people realized that they needed to understand nature and take care of natural resources; their lives depended on it.

A Faraway Place

Today, many people live in cities. They buy food in shiny supermarkets instead of growing it themselves, and their electric lights blot out the stars at night. The temperature inside their homes is always the same, no matter what the weather is like outside.

To many city children, nature seems strange. The wilderness is something that exists in an adventure movie, not in real life. Ordinarily, city children see trees and squirrels in a local park. They might spot a hawk nesting on a tall building or enjoy a few wildflowers blooming in a vacant lot. But many children have no direct experience of the wilderness with its power and beauty.

A Program in Minnesota

Across the United States, there are many programs in outdoor education for city children. One such program started in Minnesota in 2010. The program is run by a large local school system along with the National Park Service. Elementary school, middle school, and high school students are given the chance to explore the Mississippi River through both day trips and overnight camping experiences. Children learn to canoe and fish. They not only have fun; they begin to see the world through different eyes. They come to understand the environment and why they should help care for it. Then perhaps when they grow up, they will do their part to conserve natural resources.

GO ON →

From Denver to the Mountains

A similar program takes place in the mountains of Colorado. Youths from the city of Denver go to the mountains on wilderness adventures. They start out with short day hikes. If they do well, they can take part in overnight camping and more difficult activities, such as climbing. Some may even take part in trips to out-of-state places, such as Grand Teton National Park.

Many children growing up in a city like Denver have never imagined themselves climbing a mountain. At first, they find the wilderness strange and frightening. They might even find it boring because there are no TVs or electronic games. But these children learn fast. They memorize the names of birds and wildflowers. They begin to appreciate their place in protecting the wilderness and the importance of carrying out everything they bring in, such as food wrappers and water bottles. They also learn wilderness survival skills.

These children from Denver begin to see themselves as part of the natural world. Many of them decide to give back by planting trees in areas that no longer have forests or by building trails for future hikers.

GO ON →

Source #2: Urban Farming

In recent years, more people have been longing for the country life. The idea of being more self-sufficient by raising your own food is appealing to a new generation. But what happens if you can't move out to the country? Maybe you need to be close to family or work. Maybe you don't want to leave the city. In that case, you can figure out ways to bring the country life to the city.

Community Gardens

Many city neighborhoods are taking advantage of shared spaces with community gardens. Community gardens take two basic forms. First, they can be large spaces that are jointly planted, cultivated, and harvested by a community. Second, the spaces can be divided into smaller plots that people can rent. Each plot might be a ten-foot by five-foot space where a single family controls the planting, growing, and harvesting of produce. This type of plot comes in handy if the family can't plant a garden at their home.

Container Gardens

Another way to grow food in a small space is container gardening, or above-ground gardening. Any container that can hold soil and a plant can become part of a container garden. The gardener can purchase flower pots from a store or recycle objects like plastic food containers or even old tires. One advantage of container gardening is that the containers can be moved to follow sunlight. Another is that it does not require a lot of space. Window sills, patios, and balconies can all be turned into food-growing green spaces with containers.

Roof Gardens

Some creative people have made entire farms on rooftops. For example, in Brooklyn, New York, there is a rooftop farm that grows food for sale to the public. The farmers also teach people about ways to grow and prepare food, and they sell young plants to other gardeners. In Chicago, Illinois, locals can visit the first certified organic rooftop farm. It grows food used in the farm's restaurant.

Permaculture

Some home owners are taking a look at permaculture as a way of urban farming. The idea behind permaculture is to choose plants for the food they produce as well as for their beauty. Because the plants produce food each year, they become permanent parts of the landscape. This is sometimes called a food forest, which is a tiny ecosystem. In the ecosystem, the plants work together. They keep certain bugs and animals away. They also add things to the soil, such as nitrogen, that the other plants need. The plants work together, so they need much less attention

GO ON →

year after year. Plants that can be found in this type of urban farm include asparagus, rhubarb, nut or fruit trees, berry bushes, herbs, mushrooms, and even edible weeds like dandelions.

Intensive Farming

For a more traditional approach, some urban farmers are using empty lots of up to two acres to produce enough food for 200 or more families. Intensive farming uses a permanent bed system. What is planted in each bed changes every growing season. For example, in the first year, one planting bed might be planted with only garlic. The third year it might have tomatoes. The crop rotation is chosen based on what the farmer wants to grow and how many planting beds are available. The technique is based on practices that have been used in France for centuries. With intensive farming, a farmer can grow up to three times as much food as a farmer who is using a much larger space.

Urban farming is bringing some of the benefits of living in the country to people living in cities. Large spaces for farming are becoming difficult to find, so people are finding new ways to use the space they have. Any flat space, whether on the ground or on a roof, can become a garden. Urban farming is changing the way people think about farming and gardening.

GO ON →

Source #3: Basic Wilderness Survival

A leisurely walk or hike can turn into a nightmare if you become stranded and aren't prepared. Your best preparation is knowledge of basic survival needs and skills. You need water, shelter, food, and fire to survive in the wilderness.

Water

Finding a water source is a must for survival. Your body is made up of 50 to 75 percent water, depending on your age. You need to drink a gallon of water a day to survive, and you can live only three to four days without water. If you can't find a lake, river, pond, or spring, you might look to nature for help. In the desert, the flesh of a cactus can give you water. In the mountains, snow can be a source of water, but you need to melt it first. It takes ten gallons of snow to get the one gallon of water you need each day. In the forest, look for animal tracks, birds, or insects. They usually know or stay close to water sources.

When you find water, you have to make sure it is safe to drink. If you drink impure water, you could become sick, which will dry you out even faster than if you drank no water. The most certain way to purify water is to boil it for at least one minute. If you don't have a pot or your water holder might melt if placed on a fire, you can use hot rocks. Heat rocks in a fire until they are hot, and then drop them in the water to make it boil. Repeat this process as many times as needed to boil the water.

Shelter

Finding a way to protect yourself from the elements is important for survival. Sometimes you can find a natural structure, such as a cave or a rock overhang. Other times, you have to build a shelter. One easy way to start a shelter is to find a sapling, or a small, young, bendable tree. Bend the sapling and tie it down to create the shelter frame. You can use flexible branches or vines, or even blades of grass braided together, as rope. Then start attaching and overlapping leafy branches to build the sides and roof. Next, use other leafy branches to create a bed to keep you off the ground.

Food

Food is important because it gives you calories to keep going. A familiar source of calories is meat, such as beef or chicken. But if you can't find meat, nature provides alternatives. Bugs such as worms and grubs are a good source of calories. They are usually found in decaying trees and under rocks. If you can't bring yourself to eat live bugs, you can always boil them to make a stew. You can add pine needles to the water—they make a great broth and are a good source of

GO ON →

vitamin C. The new growth on pine branches can be eaten, too. Look inside pine cones for pine nuts. You can even have a dandelion salad on the side. Dandelion greens are nutritious, and the raw yellow flower is quite tasty. Another plant you can find near ponds is cattail. You can eat the entire stalk raw, and if there is pollen on the narrow flower end, you can eat that, too.

Fire

To purify water, cook food, stay warm, and even protect yourself from animals, you need fire. You could try making fire the old-fashioned way, by rubbing two sticks together until they flame up. However, it is more reliable to carry matches, a lighter, or a flint and steel kit. Pile tinder—dry twigs, leaves, grass, or paper that burns easily—in a firepit. Create a spark to light the tinder by striking the steel against the flint at an angle. Once you see smoke, the tinder has caught fire. Gently blow on the flame because fire needs oxygen to burn. Blowing on the spark feeds the fire more oxygen so it can grow and light larger logs. Just be careful not to blow so hard that you put the fire out.

The wilderness can be a harsh and unforgiving place, but with a little knowledge and practice you can survive.

GO ON →

1 Source #1 gives information about experiencing the wilderness. Select **two** details from Source #3 that give information about experiencing the wilderness that does **not** appear in Source #1.

(A) Many types of food grow naturally in the wild.

(B) People in the wilderness can catch fish for food.

(C) Wilderness survival skills can be learned quickly.

(D) Tracks of animals and birds can guide you to water.

(E) You can boil dandelion greens to make a soup to eat.

(F) Most wilderness hikers use saplings to build shelters.

2 Source #1 discusses how to introduce people who live in the city to wilderness life. Explain how the information in Source #2 adds to the reader's understanding of how city people can become comfortable outdoors. Give **two** details from Source #2 to support your explanation.

_____

_____

_____

_____

_____

_____

GO ON →

3 Explain why people sometimes have to find creative solutions to find food to eat. Give **two** reasons, one from Source #2 and one from Source #3. For each reason, include the source title or number.

_____

_____

_____

_____

_____

_____

GO ON →

Directions for Part 2

You will now look at your sources, take notes, and plan, draft, revise, and edit your narrative story for the magazine. First read your assignment and the information about how your story will be scored. Then begin your work.

Your Assignment:

Your class is creating a magazine about human survival and creativity. For your part of the magazine, you will write a narrative story that is several paragraphs long about what happens when a child from the city experiences the wilderness for the first time.

Your story will be read by parents, teachers, and the other students in your school. You should use information from multiple sources to write your narrative story. In your story, describe what happens when the city child leaves the city for the first time. When writing your narrative story, find ways to use information and details from the sources to improve your story. Make sure you develop your character(s), the setting, and the plot using details, dialogue, and description.

REMEMBER: A well-written narrative story

- has a clear plot and clear sequence of events
- is well organized and has a point of view
- uses supporting details from multiple sources
- puts the information from the sources in your own words, except when using direct quotations from the sources
- uses clear language
- follows rules of writing (spelling, punctuation, and grammar usage)

Now begin work on your narrative story. Manage your time carefully so that you can plan, write, revise, and edit the final draft of your narrative story. Write your response on a separate sheet of paper.

GO ON →

Informational Performance Task

Task:

Your class has been learning about important monuments in the United States. Now, your class is going to analyze how monuments inspire emotions in their audience. Each student will write an informational article to post on the class website.

Before deciding what to write, you do some research and find three articles about important monuments. After you have looked at these sources, you will answer some questions about them. Briefly scan the sources and answer the three questions that follow. Then, go back and read the sources carefully to gather the information you need to answer the questions and write an informational article for the class website.

In Part 2, you will write an informational article using information from the three sources.

Directions for Part 1

You will now look at three sources. You can look at any of the sources as often as you like.

Research Questions:

After looking at the sources, use the rest of the time in Part 1 to answer three questions about them. Your answers to these questions will be scored. Also, your answers will help you think about the information you have read, which should help you write your informational article. You may refer to the sources when you think it would be helpful. You may also look at your notes.

GO ON →

Source #1: The Martin Luther King, Jr. Memorial

Dr. Martin Luther King, Jr. fought for equal rights for African Americans, always favoring nonviolent means of protest. The memorial that honors this great civil rights leader opened in 2011. It is located on the National Mall in Washington, D.C., near other famous American monuments.

Dr. King was born in Atlanta in 1929. During his life, legal segregation existed in many parts of the United States. This meant that African Americans were denied jobs, education, health care, justice, and voting rights because of their race. Dr. King dedicated his life to ending these laws. He chose to fight segregation with strikes and protests instead of violence.

Many younger civil rights leaders were impatient and thought these methods were too slow. Many of his followers were hurt when they were attacked by opponents during the protests. Yet Dr. King held firm. Although he was sometimes scared, he was determined to bring lasting change through nonviolent action.

One of the high points of Dr. King's movement was the 1963 March on Washington. Near the place where his memorial would later be erected, he spoke to hundreds of thousands of Americans. He described his dreams for an America in which all people were treated equally. Not long after, the voting rights of all African Americans were guaranteed by law. In addition, segregation would soon become illegal.

NPS Photo

On April 3, 1968, Dr. King spoke to a crowd of supporters. He said, "I've seen the promised land. I may not get there with you. But I want you to know tonight that we, as a people, will get to the promised land." The next day, Dr. King was shot and killed. He gave his life to make our country better.

GO ON →

Dr. King's memorial reminds Americans to work together to achieve the promised land. As they enter, visitors are met by a 30-foot sculpture of Dr. King. The sculpture shows Dr. King with a determined expression. The sculpture grows out of the Stone of Hope. Behind this stone is another, larger one. This is the Mountain of Despair, from which the Stone of Hope was cut. Despair means "hopeless," which was how many felt before Dr. King's movement. The two stones together show that hope can arise even in times of great despair.

From the gap between the stones, visitors can see the Jefferson National Memorial, another symbol of freedom. Around the memorial winds a wall of granite. Quotations from many of Dr. King's most inspiring speeches are inscribed in the stone.

Nature plays a role in the memorial, too. Every year, cherry trees planted at the memorial bloom near the anniversary of Dr. King's death. Elm and myrtle trees also grow there. The sight and sound of flowing water give a feeling of peace. The new memorial is neither a museum nor a shrine. Instead, it is a beautiful living space and an honor to a great man.

GO ON →

Source #2: The National World War II Memorial

The National World War II Memorial stands on the National Mall in Washington, D.C. It recognizes the contributions all Americans made toward achieving victory in the war.

The first things you notice at the memorial are the 54 columns. There is one column for every state and territory in the United States at the time of World War II. These columns are linked with bronze ropes, showing how all Americans came together to support the war effort.

As you walk into the memorial, you can see the Rainbow Pool. This is a fountain with nozzles that create a perfect rainbow. The fountain was built before World War II and it was so beautiful that the architects refused to build over it. Instead, they built around it. You can admire the rainbows in the air and search the pool for reflections of the Capitol and the Washington Monument.

As you walk around the memorial, you will see brass plaques telling the story of World War II. Most plaques are based on photographs of the soldiers, workers, and medical staff who experienced the war. Some images show major battles, like Pearl Harbor and the Battle of the Bulge. Others show the home front. One shows Americans who gave money to the war effort. Another shows the women who worked in aircraft factories. Yet another shows the farmers who fed not just our troops but many British and Russian troops as well. These displays are divided by region. Those related to the war in Europe are on the north wall. Those related to the war in the Pacific are on the south wall.

The most solemn part of the memorial is the wall of stars. When you look at it, remember that each gold star represents about 100 Americans who gave their lives. Altogether, the 4,048 stars represent the more than 400,000 soldiers and civilians who were killed in the war.

If your relatives were involved in World War II, you may want to search the computerized Registry. This Registry lists all Americans who helped win the war. It includes people who lost their lives while overseas. It also includes workers and people who contributed money, food, or scrap metal to the war effort. You can look for your great-grandfather or great-grandmother! If you can't find them, you can let the memorial staff know so they can add the names to the database.

The memorial is not meant to be sad. It is a symbol of the strength of the American people when they all come together. It shows the choices and sacrifices made by the people of the United States to protect themselves and others.

GO ON →

Source #3: The Gateway Arch

The Gateway to the West, part of the Jefferson National Expansion Memorial, is a steel arch rising 630 feet over St. Louis. It honors not only Thomas Jefferson but also the westward expansion of the United States.

In 1803, President Jefferson bought the vast lands stretching from the Mississippi River to the Rocky Mountains from the French government. Then, Jefferson hired explorers Meriwether Lewis and William Clark to map the new territories. Lewis and Clark found huge plains, forests, and mountain ranges. As a result, eastern residents and new immigrants were able to travel to the West for better lives. These Americans became farmers on the plains, lumberjacks in the forests, and miners in the mountains.

The Gateway Arch represents Jefferson's effect on the United States. Because Jefferson opened the doors to the West, the arch is meant to look like a giant open gate. The size of it shows that all are welcome to come through St. Louis on the way to a better life.

Constructing the arch was difficult. The construction manager claimed that building the arch was harder than building a tower of the same height. This was because neither side of the arch supported the other until it was finished. Instead, support structures were built to prevent the two sides from falling toward each other.

When laying out the site, the engineers had to be especially careful. It was believed that the arch would fall if either side were even 1/64th of an inch off center. The lowest sections of the arch were measured over and over to make sure they were in just the right spots.

To make matters worse, no cranes were tall enough to lift the heavy metal pieces of the arch into place. Instead, the arch was built with tracks on the outside. Large elevators, called "crawlers," moved along these tracks, carrying the new pieces higher and higher. Once the new pieces were in place, workers extended the tracks so the crawlers could move even higher.

Today, visitors to the site can take elevators on the same tracks used by the crawlers. The elevators go to the very top of the arch. From this point, visitors can look west at the city of St. Louis. Beyond the city, they can see beautiful countryside. Looking east, they can see the Mississippi River. On a clear day, they can see for miles in both directions. Sadly, the observation deck windows are quite small. The pressure caused by the two halves of the arch pushing against each would shatter larger windows.

GO ON →

While at the top, visitors might be scared by a slight sway. The arch moves a couple of inches back and forth in high winds. There is no need to worry, though. The arch is designed to sway slightly to take pressure off the structure. The swaying is perfectly safe and adds a little excitement to the visit.

In addition to the slight sway, the designers also used other methods to protect the arch. The tracks and viewing platform are electrically insulated so that lightning cannot hurt the people inside. Each leg is also stuck in 26,000 tons of concrete so that it won't blow over.

The arch now stands as a reminder of the time before the West was won. Thanks to Jefferson and Americans' hard-working spirit, we not only have the West but a beautiful monument to mark it.

St. Louis arch: Barry Barker/McGraw-Hill Education

GO ON →

Name: _____ Date: _____

1 Match each source to its main topic. There will be **one** topic for **each** source.

	Source #1: The Martin Luther King, Jr. Memorial	Source #2: The National World War II Memorial	Source #3: The Gateway Arch
historical background	☐	☐	☐
construction techniques	☐	☐	☐
visitor experience	☐	☐	☐

2 Each source includes a physical description of a monument. How do these descriptions help you understand what the monuments represent? Use examples from all **three** sources to support your explanation. For each example, include the source title or number.

_____

_____

_____

_____

_____

GO ON →

Name: _____ Date: _____

3 Explain how these three different types of monuments inspire the people who visit them. Use **one** detail from **each** source to support your explanation. Be sure to give the source number or title for each detail.

_____

_____

_____

_____

_____

_____

GO ON →

Directions for Part 2

You will now look at your sources, take notes, and plan, draft, revise, and edit your article for the class website. First read your assignment and the information about how your informational article will be scored. Then begin your work.

Your Assignment:

Your class is writing papers about how monuments inspire emotion. For your part, you will compare or contrast the Gateway Arch, the Martin Luther King, Jr. Memorial, and the National World War II Memorial. Your article will be read by other students and by your teacher.

Using information from the three sources, develop a main idea comparing or contrasting how these monuments inspire emotions. Choose the most important information from more than one source to support your main idea. Then, write an informational article several paragraphs long. Clearly organize your article and support your main idea with details from the sources.

Use your own words except when quoting directly from the sources. Be sure to give the source title when using details from the sources.

REMEMBER: A well-written informational article
- has a clear main idea
- is well organized and stays on topic
- has an introduction and conclusion
- uses transitions
- uses supporting facts and details from the sources
- puts the information from the sources in your own words, except when using direct quotations from the sources
- gives the title or number of the source for the facts and details you included
- develops ideas clearly
- uses clear language
- follows the rules of writing (spelling, punctuation, and grammar usage)

Now begin work on your informational article. Manage your time carefully so that you can plan, write, revise, and edit the final draft of your informational article. Write your response on a separate sheet of paper.

GO ON →

Opinion Performance Task

Task:

Your class has been learning about how mosquitoes spread malaria and other diseases. Now, your class is going to write opinion articles, which will be published in the school newspaper, about the best way to contribute to the fight against malaria.

Before you write about the best way to help fight malaria, you do some research. As part of your research, you have found the following three sources that discuss how mosquitoes spread disease, how to treat malaria, and how countries try to beat malaria. After you have reviewed these sources, you will answer some questions about them. Briefly scan the sources and the three questions that follow. Then, go back and review the sources carefully to gather the information you will need to answer the questions and write your opinion article for the school newspaper.

In Part 2, you will write an opinion article using details from the three sources.

Directions for Part 1

You will now look at three sources. You can look at any of the sources as often as you like.

Research Questions:

After looking at the sources, use the rest of the time in Part 1 to answer three questions about them. Your answers to these questions will be scored. Also your answers will help you think about the information you have read, which should help you write your opinion article. You may refer to the sources when you think it would be helpful. You may also look at your notes.

GO ON →

Source #1: The War Against Malaria

Malaria is a disease that is carried by mosquitoes. The symptoms include fever, headache, and chills. If the disease is not treated, it can be deadly, especially in people who are very young or very old. People all over the world want to help end this dangerous disease. The most effective way to fight malaria is to distribute nets that protect people from mosquitoes.

Where and When Is Malaria Common?

Malaria is common in many parts of Africa. It is also a problem in certain parts of South Asia, the Middle East, and Latin America. In 2010, 225 million cases of this disease were reported around the world. The good news is that, in some countries, malaria has been eliminated. For example, Morocco in northwestern Africa is now free of this disease.

Because malaria is carried by mosquitoes, and because mosquitoes breed in water, malaria is more common during the rainy season. Also, most malaria-carrying mosquitoes bite at night, so that is the time when people need to protect themselves.

How Can Malaria Be Fought?

Malaria can be fought in a number of ways. Some people believe that developing a malaria vaccine is the best way. A vaccine is a type of medicine that prevents a person from getting a disease. Today, there is no workable vaccine against malaria. However, several organizations are currently studying possible vaccines. Vaccines have helped control other diseases, such as polio and measles. Someday soon there may be a safe vaccine to prevent malaria, too. But the world needs ways to fight against malaria in the meantime.

For those who become ill with malaria, there is treatment. Individuals who show symptoms, or signs, of the disease are first given a test. The test provides results very quickly. If the person actually has malaria, he or she is treated with a group of medicines called ACT.

The best way to fight malaria is to keep people from getting sick in the first place. One approach is to spray insect-killing chemicals, or insecticides, in houses. An even better method is for people to sleep under an insecticide-treated mosquito net, or ITN. A chemical that kills mosquitoes is applied to this kind of tent. The people sleeping under ITNs are safe from mosquito bites. ITNs are currently the best way to fight malaria. They are a simple, inexpensive way to prevent malaria in the first place.

GO ON →

Malaria Fighters

The United Nations has been fighting malaria for years. Today, governments and charities all over the world are distributing ITNs to people in need. They are helping people protect themselves from mosquito bites so they do not become sick.

One day doctors may develop a vaccine to prevent malaria, but that could be years away. In the meantime, people can best fight the disease by donating an ITN to people at risk of getting malaria. The nets do not cost much, and they can make a big difference by saving lives.

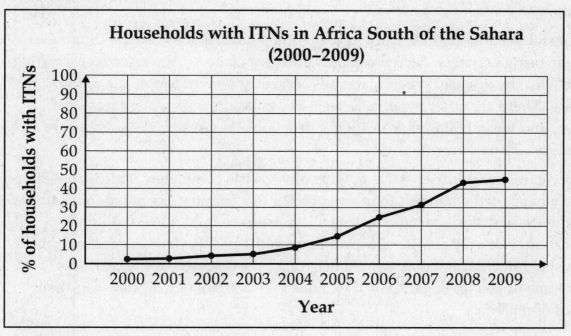

Households with ITNs in Africa South of the Sahara (2000–2009)

GO ON →

Source #2: A Malaria-Free World

Malaria used to be a worldwide problem. In 1945, the disease was prevalent around the globe, except in northern countries like Norway, Sweden, and Iceland. Today, malaria has been wiped out in North America, Europe, and Australia. However, it still rages in some areas of Africa, China, the Middle East, and Latin America.

The ideal, of course, is to destroy the disease completely, but many countries do not have the resources to win that long, difficult, expensive battle. The best they can do is to control the disease.

To control malaria, nations work to prevent most cases of the illness. Strategies include using bed nets, decreasing mosquito populations, and effectively treating those with the disease. When malaria is controlled, fewer people die of the disease. There are other benefits as well. Fewer adults miss work because of illness, and fewer children are kept out of school. As a result, these countries fare better socially and economically.

However, many countries strive to wipe out malaria completely. This is considered to have happened when less than one percent of a country's population is infected. Getting rid of malaria means treating all cases—even mild ones—with great dedication. Not only are the sick people treated, but their families and neighbors are tested for malaria. Some people may carry the disease but may not show any symptoms or feel ill. Regardless, they must take a series of drugs to clear their bodies of malaria.

There are complications to this process, though. The most common malaria strain in these countries is called *Plasmodium vivax*. This strain of parasite can live inactive in the liver for years. It is more difficult to detect this inactive form of malaria. Also, the drug used to treat it can be fatal in some cases. A safer solution is to space the drug dosages out over two weeks. However, some people object to taking the medicine in the first place because they do not feel sick. Without cooperation from its citizens, a country cannot effectively beat malaria.

Even when a country becomes malaria-free, it must still keep watch for new cases. People visiting from other countries may bring malaria with them. Thus, countries must always keep control measures in place to prevent an outbreak of the disease.

GO ON →

Despite these problems, countries like to say that they have beaten malaria. Tourism often flourishes in malaria-free countries, in contrast to those still struggling with the disease.

Some scientists believe that malaria can one day be completely wiped out across the globe. But until then, countries have to look at the situation realistically. While they may wish to destroy malaria quickly, they must understand that the process is unfortunately not so simple.

GO ON →

Source #3: Mosquitoes

It's a scenario most people are familiar with. On a warm summer evening, as everyone is enjoying the outdoors, a pesky mosquito lands on a bare arm or leg. Its needlelike mouth pierces the skin. Then the mosquito flies away—or gets swatted by an annoyed human—leaving a raised, itchy bump on the skin.

Mosquito bites are annoying but mostly harmless, right? For most people in the United States, this is the reality. But in some other areas of the world, mosquitoes carry more risk than a temporary itchy bump. In fact, they are known to carry and spread diseases such as yellow fever, malaria, and West Nile virus.

Little Fly

Mosquitoes get their name from the Spanish for "little fly." The term is appropriate because they are part of the fly family. Generally, it is the female mosquito that sucks the blood of other creatures with her mouth. And humans aren't the only target. Mosquitoes also suck the blood of other mammals, birds, reptiles, and amphibians. Even some fish are not safe from mosquito bites!

It is hard to avoid mosquitoes. At least some species of mosquitoes are present on every continent except Antarctica. Some extremely cold islands like Iceland also have no mosquitoes. In temperate zones, mosquitoes mostly appear in the humid summer months. They hibernate during the winter. However, tropical areas may have mosquitoes 365 days of the year.

Feeding Habits

The mouths of mosquitoes are shaped like a skinny tube, perfect for piercing the skin and sucking blood. However, these mouths are also useful for drinking sugary substances like honeydew and nectar. Male mosquitoes drink only these sweet fluids. Females, on the other hand, have their choice of blood or sugar. Sugar gives them energy, while blood gives them the protein needed to produce eggs.

Vectors of Disease

Some species of mosquitoes are known as *vectors of disease,* which means they carry and pass on diseases to other creatures. Each year, mosquitoes spread diseases to millions of people in Africa, Russia, Asia, South America, and Central America.

Health organizations constantly work to prevent these diseases from spreading. Their strategies include decreasing mosquito populations, developing vaccines and medications, and passing out sleeping nets. Because mosquitoes gather around stagnant water, people can get rid of mosquitoes by removing these habitats. People can also combat mosquitoes by introducing dragonflies and certain types of fish into the environment. These animals are natural predators of the mosquito.

GO ON →

Mosquito nets are particularly effective at protecting people from mosquito bites in regions where the risk of disease is high. The nets are treated with an insecticide that kills mosquitoes. People drape these nets over their beds to protect themselves while they sleep.

Mosquito bites are a minor bother to some people, and a serious health risk to others. Until doctors can develop effective treatments for diseases caused by mosquitoes, controlling mosquito populations will remain a major struggle.

GO ON →

1 Draw a line between each source and the idea it supports.

| Source #1: The War Against Malaria | | Destroying malaria is a complicated and costly struggle. |

| Source #2: A Malaria-Free World | | Mosquitoes exist all over the world except for some very cold regions. |

| Source #3: Mosquitoes | | People most need to protect themselves from malaria during the rainy season. |

2 The sources discuss how malaria is spread and fought. Explain what the sources say about fighting malaria. Use **one** detail from each source to support your explanation. For each detail, include the source title or number.

_____

_____

_____

_____

_____

_____

GO ON →

3 Source #1 includes a graph. Explain how this graph would be helpful if it were added to Source #2. Give **two** details from Source #2 to support your explanation.

_____

_____

_____

_____

_____

_____

GO ON →

Directions for Part 2

You will now look at your sources, take notes, and plan, draft, revise, and edit your opinion article. First read your assignment and the information about how your opinion article will be scored. Then begin your work.

Your Assignment:

Your class is writing opinion articles about fighting malaria for the school newspaper. For your article, you will write an argument that is several paragraphs long about whether it is better to donate money for ITNs or for malaria vaccine research.

Your opinion article will be read by parents, teachers, and the other students in your school. You should use information from multiple sources to write your article. In your article, describe how ITNs and vaccines would help people at risk of getting malaria. When writing your opinion article, find ways to use information and details from the sources to strengthen your argument.

REMEMBER: A well-written opinion article

- has a clear opinion
- is well-organized and stays on the topic
- has an introduction and conclusion
- uses transitions
- uses details or facts from multiple sources to support your opinion
- puts the information from the sources in your own words, except when using direct quotations from the sources
- gives the name or number of the source for the details or facts you included
- develops ideas clearly
- uses clear language
- follows the rules of writing (spelling, punctuation, and grammar usage)

Now begin work on your opinion article. Manage your time carefully so that you can plan, write, revise, and edit the final draft of your opinion article. Write your response on a separate sheet of paper.

GO ON →

Name: _____

Question	Correct Answer	Content Focus	CCSS	Complexity
BENCHMARK ASSESSMENT—TEST 1				
1A	A	Context Clues: Sentence Clues	L.5.4a	DOK 2
1B	D	Context Clues: Sentence Clues/Text Evidence	L.5.4a/ RL.5.1	DOK 2
2	see below	Character, Setting, Plot: Compare and Contrast	RL.5.3	DOK 3
3A	A	Theme	RL.5.2	DOK 2
3B	B	Theme/Text Evidence	RL.5.2/ RL.5.1	DOK 2
4	see below	Character, Setting, Plot: Compare and Contrast	RL.5.3	DOK 3
5	A	Character, Setting, Plot: Compare and Contrast	RL.5.3	DOK 2
6A	B	Simile and Metaphor	L.5.5a	DOK 2
6B	C	Simile and Metaphor/Text Evidence	L.5.5a/ RI.5.1	DOK 3
7	A	Text Structure: Cause and Effect	RI.5.3	DOK 3
8	B, D	Context Clues: Definitions and Restatement	L.5.4a	DOK 2
9	D, E, F	Greek and Latin Roots	L.5.4b	DOK 2
10A	C	Text Structure: Cause and Effect	RI.5.3	DOK 2
10B	A	Text Structure: Cause and Effect/Text Evidence	RI.5.3/ RI.5.1	DOK 2
11A	C	Author's Point of View	RI.5.8	DOK 3
11B	D	Author's Point of View/Text Evidence	RI.5.8/ RI.5.1	DOK 2
12A	D	Main Idea and Key Details	RI.5.2	DOK 2
12B	D	Main Idea and Key Details/Text Evidence	RI.5.2/ RI.5.1	DOK 2
13	B	Text Structure: Cause and Effect	RI.5.3	DOK 2
14	A, D	Research	W.5.8, RI.5.6, RI.5.1	DOK 2
15	D,F	Research	W.5.8, RI.5.1, RI.5.7, RI.5.9	DOK 3
16	C	Research	W.5.8, RI.5.7, RI.5.1,	DOK 2
17	C	Research	W.5.8	DOK 2

BENCHMARK ASSESSMENT—TEST 1

Question	Correct Answer	Content Focus	CCSS	Complexity
18	see below	Informational: Drafting, Editing, Revising	W.5.2a	DOK 3
19	B	Opinion: Drafting, Editing, Revising	W.5.1a	DOK 2
20	D	Narrative: Drafting, Editing, Revising	W.5.3a	DOK 2
21A	D	Context Clues: Sentence Clues	L.5.5a	DOK 2
21B	A	Context Clues: Sentence Clues/Text Evidence	L.5.5a/ RL.5.1	DOK 2
22	C	Character, Setting, Plot: Sequence	RL.3.3	DOK 2
23	A, D	Idioms	L.5.5b	DOK 2
24A	C	Context Clues: Sentence Clues	L.5.5a	DOK 2
24B	C	Context Clues: Sentence Clues/Text Evidence	L.5.5a/ RL.5.1	DOK 2
25A	A	Idioms	L.5.5b	DOK 2
25B	C	Idioms/Text Evidence	L.5.5b/ RL.5.1	DOK 2
26A	C	Theme	RL.5.2	DOK 2
26B	C	Theme/Text Evidence	RL.5.2/ RL.5.1	DOK 2
27A	A	Character, Setting, Plot: Problem and Solution	RL.4.3	DOK 2
27B	D	Character, Setting, Plot: Problem and Solution/Text Evidence	RL.4.3/ RL.5.1	DOK 2
28	see below	Theme	RL.5.2	DOK 2
29A	B	Author's Point of View	RI.5.8	DOK 2
29B	D	Author's Point of View/Text Evidence	RI.5.8/ RI.5.1	DOK 2
30	C	Sentence Clues; Definitions and Restatement	L.5.4a	DOK 2
31A	C	Text Structure: Cause and Effect	RI.5.3	DOK 2
31B	D	Text Structure: Cause and Effect/Text Evidence	RI.5.3/ RI.5.1	DOK 2
32	See below	Main Idea and Key Details	RI.5.2	DOK 2
33A	C	Main Idea and Key Details	RI.5.2	DOK 2
33B	C	Main Idea and Key Details/Text Evidence	RI.5.2/ RI.5.1	DOK 2
34	C	Verb Tenses	L5.1b	DOK 1
35	A, C	Compound Sentences and Conjunctions	L5.1e	DOK 2

BENCHMARK ASSESSMENT—TEST 1

Question	Correct Answer	Content Focus	CCSS	Complexity
36	B	Verb Tenses	L5.1c	DOK 2
37	D	Revising	W.5.3d	DOK 2
38	B	Revising	W.5.2d	DOK 2
39	D	Revising	W.5.2d	DOK 2

Comprehension: Selected Response 2, 3A, 3B, 5, 7, 9A, 9B, 10A, 10B, 11A, 11B, 12A, 12B, 13, 22, 26A, 26B, 27A, 27B, 29A, 29B, 31A, 31B, 32, 33A, 33B	/32	%
Comprehension: Constructed Response 4, 28	/4	%
Vocabulary 1A, 1B, 6A, 6B, 8, 21A, 21B, 23, 24A, 24B, 25A, 25B, 30	/16	%
Research 14, 15, 16, 17	/8	%
Drafting, Editing, Revising 18, 19, 20, 37, 38, 39	/12	%
English Language Conventions 34, 35, 36	/6	%
Total Benchmark Assessment Score	/78	%

2 Students should match the following: Shakira: Willing to overcome problems to get what she wants; Shakira's mother: worried about the challenges of raising pickles; Zoe: able to make hard choices to keep Pickles forever.

4 **2-point response:** Shakira has always wanted a dog, but moves too frequently to have one. Zoe has to move to another country temporarily and must give up her dog. They come up with a plan, and Shakira's mother is convinced to allow her to take care of the dog while Zoe is away. *Sacrificing* means to give up something. Shakira's mother uses this word to describe how a soldier gives up things for her country. She says she would be "proud to help" Zoe's mother. This shows that Shakira's mother really appreciates Zoe's mother's military service.

18 **2-point response:** Dentists recommend you brush and floss every day. Brush your teeth twice a day, thirty minutes after eating. Use a soft toothbrush and a drop of toothpaste. Flossing gets rid of plaque and food and stops buildup of tartar. Tartar is plaque that hardens on the teeth over time.

Eating well and visiting the dentist are other ways to protect teeth. Sugary foods produce acids in the mouth that damage teeth. You should avoid candy, or brush your teeth afterwards. Visit your dentist every six months, who will clean your teeth, remove any plaque and tartar, and find any cavities.

28 **2-point response:** In the story "Ant Farm," after Murphy's dad was unable to use his excavator, Murphy felt an ant tickling his leg to get attention. He bent down to get a better view of the ant, and saw it was trying to tell him a better location to begin the digging. Since ants do not behave this way, and cannot communicate with people, we know that this is not realistic fiction.

32 Students should match the following: deer: two toes in front, two toes in back; fox: four toes in front, four toes in back; squirrel: four toes in front, five toes in back; fisher: five toes in front, five toes in back.

Answer Key

Name: _____

BENCHMARK ASSESSMENT—TEST 2				
Question	**Correct Answer**	**Content Focus**	**CCSS**	**Complexity**
1A	B	Context Clues: Paragraph Clues	L.5.4a	DOK 2
1B	D	Context Clues: Paragraph Clues/Text Evidence	L.5.4a/ RL.5.1	DOK 2
2A	A	Character, Setting, Plot: Compare and Contrast	RL.5.3	DOK 3
2B	A	Character, Setting, Plot: Compare and Contrast/Text Evidence	RL.5.3/ RL.5.1	DOK 2
3	see below	Point of View	RL.5.6	DOK 2
4A	D	Character, Setting, Plot: Sequence	RL.5.3	DOK 2
4B	D	Character, Setting, Plot: Sequence/Text Evidence	RL.5.3/ RL.5.1	DOK 2
5	see below	Theme	RL.5.2	DOK 2
6	A, D	Text Structure: Sequence	RI.5.5	DOK 3
7A	C	Context Clues: Sentence Clues	L.5.4a	DOK 2
7B	D	Context Clues: Sentence Clues/Text Evidence	L.5.4a/ RI.5.1	DOK 2
8A	A	Context Clues: Sentence Clues	L.5.4a	DOK 2
8B	B	Context Clues: Sentence Clues/Text Evidence	L.5.4a/ RI.5.1	DOK 2
9A	D	Main Idea and Key Details	RI.5.2	DOK 2
9B	C	Main Idea and Key Details/Text Evidence	RI.5.2/ RI.5.1	DOK 2
10	D	Author's Point of View	RI.5.8	DOK 2
11A	A	Text Structure: Cause and Effect	RI.5.3	DOK 2
11B	D	Text Structure: Cause and Effect/Text Evidence	RI.5.3/ RI.5.1	DOK 2
12A	A	Author's Point of View	RI.5.8	DOK 3
12B	D	Author's Point of View /Text Evidence	RI.5.8/ RI.5.1	DOK 3
13	see below	Main Idea and Key Details	RI.5.2	DOK 3
14	B, E	Research	W.5.8	DOK 2
15	C, F	Research	W.5.8	DOK 2
16	A	Research	W.5.8	DOK 2
17	A	Research	W.5.8	DOK 2
18	see below	Opinion: Drafting, Editing, Revising	W.5.1d	DOK 3

Answer Key

Name: _____

BENCHMARK ASSESSMENT—TEST 2				
Question	Correct Answer	Content Focus	CCSS	Complexity
19	D	Narrative: Drafting, Editing, Revising	W.5.3b	DOK 2
20	A	Informational: Drafting, Editing, Revising	W.5.2c	DOK 2
21A	D	Proverbs and Adages	L.5.5b	DOK 2
21B	B	Proverbs and Adages/Text Evidence	L.5.5b/ RL.5.1	DOK 2
22A	B	Character, Setting, Plot: Sequence	RL.4.3	DOK 2
22B	B	Character, Setting, Plot: Sequence/Text Evidence	RL.4.3/ RL.5.1	DOK 2
23A	D	Connotation and Denotation	L.5.5	DOK 2
23B	A	Connotation and Denotation/Text Evidence	L.5.5/ RI.5.1	DOK 2
24	C, F	Character, Setting, Plot: Sequence	RL.5.3	DOK 2
25A	B	Theme	RL.5.2	DOK 2
25B	D	Theme/Text Evidence	RL.5.2/ RL.5.1	DOK 2
26	C, F	Theme	RL.5.2	DOK 2
27	see below	Character, Setting, Plot: Compare and Contrast	RL.5.3	DOK 3
28	see below	Character, Setting, Plot: Problem and Solution	RL.4.3	DOK 2
29A	A	Author's Point of View	RI.5.8	DOK 3
29B	B	Author's Point of View /Text Evidence	RI.5.8/ RI.5.1	DOK 2
30A	B	Context Clues: Sentence Clues	L.5.4a	DOK 2
30B	B	Context Clues: Sentence Clues/Text Evidence	L.5.4a/ RI.5.1	DOK 2
31	B, C, E	Main Idea and Key Details	RI.5.2	DOK 3
32	B	Author's Point of View	RI.5.8	DOK 3
33	B	Text Feature: Chart	RI.4.7	DOK 3
34	C, F	Complex Sentences	L.5.2b	DOK 2
35	A	Verb Tenses	L.5.1c	DOK 1
36	B	Compound Sentences and Conjunctions	L.5.1a	DOK 2

Name: _____

BENCHMARK ASSESSMENT—TEST 2

Question	Correct Answer	Content Focus	CCSS	Complexity
37	D, F	Revising	W.5.1	DOK 2
38	D	Revising	W.5.1	DOK 1
39	C	Revising	W.5.1	DOK 1

Comprehension: Selected Response 2A, 2B, 4, 6, 9A, 9B, 10, 11A, 11B, 12A, 12B, 22A, 22B, 24, 25A, 25B, 26, 27, 29A, 29B, 31, 32, 33		/32	%
Comprehension: Constructed Response 3, 5, 13, 28		/8	%
Vocabulary 1A, 1B, 7A, 7B, 8A, 8B, 21A, 21B, 23A, 23B, 30A, 30B		/12	%
Research 14, 15, 16, 17		/8	%
Drafting, Editing, Revising 18, 19, 20, 37, 38, 39		/12	%
English Language Conventions 34, 35, 36		/6	%
Total Benchmark Assessment Score		/78	%

3 Students should match the following: Nina is anxious about being Fiona's friend: The new girl looked a little lost, so I decided to go out on a limb and introduce myself; Fiona is concerned about the feeling of others: She squeezed in to make room for me, too; Nina has a difficult time expressing herself: I really liked Fiona, but sometimes I felt a little left out.

5 **2-point response:** The story is about a girl named Fiona who comes to a new school from England. The narrator, Nina, and her friend Audrey become friends with Fiona. Nina has trouble understanding Fiona because her version of English is different than American English. Audrey, however, can understand Fiona because her mother is from England. This puts stress on Nina and Audrey's friendship. "Stop acting like such a know-it-all, Audrey!" Nina yells. In the end, all three girls decide to remain friends and make a dictionary so they can understand each other easily.

13 **2-point response:** Marie Curie was determined to succeed even when facing hardships: Even though she was often sick during this period, she complete her work in only three years; Scientific discoveries can have a positive impact on the lives of others: A brand-new medical technique called the X ray was invented, and a scientist was able to bring the invention to the battlefield.

18 **2-point response:** If fifth graders could ride their bikes, they would have improved fitness and concentration in class. The school would benefit too, because the fifth graders would become better students and do better in class. The school could save money and help the environment at the same time. As you can see, the pros of letting us ride our bikes to and from school outweigh the cons. For these reasons, please consider approving this idea.

27 Students should match the following: Abby: discouraged, determined to help others, creates change, persuades someone to try something new; Greta: discouraged, misses someone close to them, confused by new technology.

28 **2-point response:** Abby overcame her feelings by finding a new way to help, and by succeeding despite challenges like the low attendance at her class. Greta helped Abby overcome these feelings by accepting help and convincing others, like Susan, to accept it as well.

Answer Key

Name: _____

Narrative Performance Task				
Question	**Answer**	**CCSS**	**Complexity**	**Score**
1	A, D		DOK 2	/1
2	see below	RI.5.1, RI.5.7, RI.5.9 W.5.2, W.5.3a–e, W.5.4, W.5.7, W.5.8 L.5.1, L.5.2	DOK 3	/2
3	see below		DOK 3	/2
Narrative Story	see below		DOK 4	/4 [P/O] /4 [D/E] /2 [C]
Total Score				/15

2 **2-point response:** Source #1 tells about connecting people with nature and describes several programs that help students become comfortable in the wilderness. Source #2 discusses creative ways to bring nature to the city in the form of growing food. One example it uses is a rooftop vegetable farm in New York City. It also points out that "many city neighborhoods are taking advantage of shared spaces with community gardens." This helps the reader understand how people can connect with nature without leaving the city.

3 **2-point response:** Sometimes people who live in cities want fresh, natural food. This can be a challenge. Source #2 describes creative solutions that city people have found. They have made gardens and even whole farms on the roofs of buildings because space is limited. Sometimes people must be creative about finding food for other reasons. Source #3 describes what people need to know to survive in the wilderness. For example, it suggests boiling worms and slugs to make a stew. It also explains that following animal tracks can help a person find water.

10-point anchor paper: "I am so excited to go on my first camping trip," Natalie thought as the bus pulled away from her elementary school. Living in Denver, she had always seen mountains, but now she was going to do more than just see them.

"Natalie, you look like you're about to explode!" Madge said. Natalie smiled. Madge had been her friend since second grade.

Natalie took a deep breath and exclaimed, "I am! And the only person I would ever want with me when I leave the city for the first time is my best friend!"

Madge smiled and gave Natalie a hug. The next few hours whizzed by, until the bus finally came to a stop in a parking lot near a campsite.

Mrs. Chandler, Natalie's science teacher, stood in the front of the bus and gave directions. The only thing Natalie heard was, "Okay, everybody off the bus."

Madge and Natalie grabbed their bags from the storage space beneath the bus and scouted out their space in paradise. "I like this spot," Madge said. "What do you think?"

Without really looking, Natalie quickly responded, "Looks great. Let's go explore now."

"But we have to set up our tent first," Madge said, pointing to the small blue sack that lay on the ground. "We should do that first and then we can explore to our heart's content."

Natalie frowned, "But I have watched soooo many survival shows, and they always explore their surroundings first before setting up a tent. Let's just take a few minutes, please," Natalie begged.

"Oh, all right." Madge barely had time to grab her water bottle before Natalie had whisked her off on their adventure. They had been walking about 15 minutes when they started to hear running water.

"Do you hear that?" Natalie whispered. "Let's follow the sound." Both girls were now caught up in the excitement of the trip, so Madge quickly agreed.

There was so much to look at and hear. Natalie loved it. She thought about her last class trip to see a rooftop farm in Denver. It was interesting and gave her an idea about what farming was like, but it was nothing like being out here in the wilderness of the Rocky Mountains. There was no traffic noise or smell here like on the rooftop, Natalie thought, just the smell of fresh air and the sound of branches.

Cracking branches.

Natalie stopped short.

It took Madge a few seconds to realize she was walking by herself. "Why did you stop?"

"SHHHHHH!"

"Why are you shushing me?"

"Get over here!" Natalie whispered urgently. "Did you hear that?" She grabbed her friend's arm.

"Hear what?"

Crack. Snap.

Both girls looked at each other. "What-what is that?"

"I don't know. You're the one who was supposed to have watched all those survival shows."

The noise was getting louder and closer. In another instant, Natalie yelled, "RUN!"

Both girls took off running blindly through the trees. After a while, Natalie turned her head to look backward while she was running. Before she could turn back frontward, her head smacked into a low tree branch. The force knocked her off her feet, and everything went black.

Several hours passed before Natalie woke up lying on the forest floor. She took off her glasses and looked around. Where was Madge? Was it a bear she had heard? Did it get Madge? One question finally blocked out all the others: "Where am I?"

Panic rose in Natalie's throat as she scanned the forest for something familiar. Nothing. The water, she thought. She held her breath when she realized she could not hear the water anymore. She hugged her knees and buried her face in her arms. She was lost.

After a few panicked tears, Natalie gathered her thoughts. To survive, she needed water. She felt along her belt and then realized it was Madge who had grabbed the water bottle, not her.

"I have to find water," she said, and pulled herself to her feet. "Animal tracks," she remembered. "I have to find animal tracks. They always know where to find water." She looked around for animal tracks. After a few minutes, she saw a deer trail and followed it. She hoped it was leading toward water and not away from it. Natalie walked for what seemed like forever when she finally heard flowing water.

She reached the edge of a creek and was about to take a drink of water when she remembered she should boil the water for safety. But how? She almost started running, but the throbbing of her head told her walking was a safer choice.

Her glasses. She could use her glasses to start a fire, but she would have to start soon. She had to get wood before the sun set.

She had gathered more wood than she could carry when she saw something that made her jump for joy—dandelions. At that moment, she realized how hungry she felt. She reached down and picked the plants, ate a few yellow blossoms, and put the rest in her pocket.

She smiled as she stacked her branches and dry grass to start her fire. She used the lens of her glasses to focus the sun on a piece of tissue she found in her pocket. She held the lens and waited, but nothing happened. She looked at the sky and her heart sank. It would be dark soon. She had no fire, no water, and no shelter. She leaned back against a tree and closed her eyes. What was she going to do now? She ate a few more dandelion blossoms and decided she had to find shelter. She stood, brushed off her pants, took a few steps, and stopped.

What was that? Her heart beat faster. Voices! She relaxed as Madge and Mrs. Chandler approached from the other side of the tree.

Informational Performance Task				
Question	**Answer**	**CCSS**	**Complexity**	**Score**
1	see below	RI.5.1, RI.5.7, RI.5.9 W.5.2a-e, W.5.4, W.5.7, W.5.8, W.5.9b L.5.1, L.5.2	DOK 2	/1
2	see below		DOK 3	/2
3	see below		DOK 3	/2
Informational Article	see below		DOK 4	/4 [P/O] /4 [E/E] /2 [C]
Total Score				**/15**

1 Students should match the following:
  • Source #1: The Martin Luther King, Jr. Memorial – historical background
  • Source #2: The National World War II Memorial – visitor experience
  • Source #3: The Gateway Arch – construction techniques

2 **2-point response:** Source #1 describes how the monument represents the persistence and cooperation needed to overcome life's challenges. The monument includes a sculpture of a determined-looking Dr. King coming out of the Stone of Hope, which was cut from a larger stone that represents the Mountain of Despair. The description of the World War II Memorial in Source #2 illustrates how fountain, plaques, and columns all work together to tell the story of the war and the people it affected. In Source #3, the challenges involved in building the Gateway Arch were great, and so were the challenges faced by the people who passed through St. Louis, the Gateway to the West, on their way to a better life.

3 **2-point response:** Source #1 explains that the King memorial is a place of hope and inspiration, a physical reminder that "hope can arise in times of great despair." Source #2 points out that the memorial is not supposed to be sad; it is a place where visitors can learn about different aspects of World War II and reflect on the contributions made by so many people working together even while doing different jobs in different places. In Source #3, the "giant open gate" that forms the Gateway Arch can make visitors feel proud of hard-working American spirit that helped the country grow.

10-point anchor paper: People who design monuments to great people and events try hard to inspire emotions. They do this so that visitors to the monuments will feel a stronger connection to their subjects. Sometimes the emotions come from the monument itself, and sometimes they come from the surroundings. Three good examples are the Gateway Arch in St. Louis and the Martin Luther King, Jr. Memorial and National World War II Memorial in Washington, D.C.

The Gateway Arch is affected by geography. It frames St. Louis and the distant plains like a gate. This helps visitors feel what the pioneers heading to the West must have felt in the 1800s. According to Source #3, it also has a viewing platform at the top, with windows looking both east and west. These windows let visitors see where the pioneers came from and where they were going. Because the windows are so high, visitors can also feel wonder at how large and open the lands west of the Mississippi River are. Both the appearance of the arch from the outside and the view from the inside use the surroundings to help viewers feel that the West was grand and exciting.

The Martin Luther King, Jr. Memorial is much smaller, but it relies on its surroundings even more. Source #1 explains that the memorial is a symbol of freedom, change, and hope. It notes that a gap in the Mountain of Despair in the King Memorial is positioned to give a view of the Jefferson Memorial, another famous symbol of freedom, change, and hope. The source also mentions the importance of nature to the King Memorial. The memorial is not walled in. Instead, it is the focal point of a park, strengthening the feeling of freedom. The nearby trees and beautiful wide-open space inspire feelings of peace and may be like the "promised land" that Dr. King wanted in life. The cherry trees that bloom near the anniversary of Dr. King's death inspire hope for a new beginning. By using the surroundings, the designers created a monument that is very effective at inspiring hope, freedom, and peace.

The National World War II Memorial is less open than the others. Two walls separate the monument from the rest of the National Mall. This makes visitors focus more on the monument and less on the surroundings. However, the designers used the Rainbow Pool, which is an older feature that was already on the site. The Rainbow Pool adds beauty and peace, making the mood less solemn. In Source #2, the writer states that a visitor can see reflections of the Washington Monument and the Capitol in the pool. This enables people see America standing tall, despite the sacrifices, and helps them feel thankful.

All three monuments use their environment to inspire emotion. The Gateway Arch shows off the wide spaces of Missouri, the Martin Luther King, Jr. Memorial uses the surrounding trees and the Jefferson Memorial to inspire hope, and the National World War II Memorial uses the reflections of other monuments to inspire thankfulness. This shows that the emotions inspired by monuments result not only from how the structures look but also from how they fit into the landscape.

Opinion Performance Task				
Question	**Answer**	**CCSS**	**Complexity**	**Score**
1	see below	RI.5.1, RI.5.7, RI.5.9 W.5.1a-d, W.5.2, W.5.4, W.5.7, W.5.8 L.5.1, L.5.2	DOK 2	/1
2	see below		DOK 3	/2
3	see below		DOK 4	/2
Opinion Article	see below		DOK 4	/4 [P/O] /4 [E/E] /2 [C]
Total Score				**/15**

1 Students should match the following:
- Source #1: The War Against Malaria – People most need to protect themselves from malaria during the rainy season.
- Source #2: A Malaria-Free World – Destroying malaria is a complicated and costly struggle.
- Source #3: Mosquitoes – Mosquitoes exist all over the world except for some very cold regions.

2 **2-point response:** According to Source #1, doctors are trying to make a malaria vaccine, but in the meantime there are medicines called ACT and insecticide-treated mosquito nets (ITNs). Source #2 says that countries try to wipe out malaria by testing the friends and family of those infected for malaria and treating people with medicine even if they don't feel sick. Source #3 says that decreasing mosquito populations can decrease malaria. People can remove stagnant water and introduce predators to the environment to do this.

3 **2-point response:** According to Source #2, parts of Africa have a high risk of malaria. This source also describes how many countries try to prevent the disease, including using bed nets (ITNs) to prevent mosquitoes from biting. By preventing the disease, fewer adults and children miss work or school. The graph from Source #1 supports the information in Source #2 because it shows that the percentage of southern African households with ITNs increased to almost 50% from 2000 to 2009. It gives readers a quick and easy way to see how efficient this method of prevention can be.

10-point anchor paper: Malaria is a serious disease that affects millions of people around the world. The disease can be deadly if not treated. Fortunately, there are ways to avoid getting the disease. Because malaria is spread by mosquitoes, people can avoid malaria by sleeping under insecticide-treated mosquito nets, or ITNs. The best way to join the fight against malaria is to donate ITNs to countries where malaria is a problem.

According to Source #1 and Source #2, malaria is a serious problem in parts of Africa, Latin America, South Asia, and the Middle East. In 2010, according to Source #1, there were 225 million cases of malaria around the world. Health organizations are working to create a vaccine for malaria, but so far none have been successful. Donating money to vaccine research would be a good cause to help people in the future, but people need help to stop the spread of malaria right now.

Source #3 explains that mosquitoes pass on malaria to other people and animals. It also says that nets treated with insecticide are very effective at protecting people from mosquitoes. People sleep under the nets because mosquitoes are most active in the evenings and at night. According to Source #1, ITNs are "a simple, inexpensive way to prevent malaria in the first place."

Because ITNs are a simple and inexpensive solution, it is easy to convince more people to donate to the cause. Just by sleeping under a net, men, women, and children can avoid getting mosquito bites and getting sick. They won't have to miss school or work, and they won't have to take a series of medicines to treat malaria. The best way to fight malaria is to keep people from getting it at all. Donating ITNs is the best way to make that happen and to save lives.